Critical Legal Studies and the Campaign
for American Law Schools

Paul Baumgardner

Critical Legal Studies and the Campaign for American Law Schools

A Revolution to Break the Liberal Consensus

Paul Baumgardner
College of Interdisciplinary Studies & Global Education
Belmont University
Nashville, TN, USA

ISBN 978-3-030-82377-1   ISBN 978-3-030-82378-8   (eBook)
https://doi.org/10.1007/978-3-030-82378-8

Cover ilustration: © Melisa Hasan

This Palgrave Macmillan imprint is published by the registered company Springer Nature Switzerland AG
The registered company address is: Gewerbestrasse 11, 6330 Cham, Switzerland

Acknowledgments

The years spent researching the CLS movement and the politics of the 1980s legal academy were full of excitement and wonder. I will be forever grateful to those who have helped me during this time.

This book would not have been possible without the kindness of many people. At Princeton University, I received an abundance of support and guidance from Dirk Hartog, Keith Whittington, Brooke Holmes, and Steve Macedo. Above all, I would like to thank Paul Frymer, who was too generous with his time and his wisdom as I moved through this research. He was the best dissertation chair that a graduate student could ask for, and he spent years going above and beyond for me.

At the American Bar Foundation, I was welcomed and aided by the greatest of scholars, including Ajay Mehrotra, Stephen Daniels, Terence Halliday, Jothie Rajah, and Christopher Schmidt. Beth Mertz, in particular, was always there when I needed a friend and a mentor. One day, I hope to become as good of a scholar and a colleague as Beth.

Laurette Liesen, you understood what I was going through as a first-time teacher, and you taught me more than you know about being a professor, a political scientist, and a decent human being.

Jerold Waltman, you did more than anyone to set me on this academic path and to demonstrate scholarly care. You are a remarkable thinker, teacher, and friend. Thank you.

To my parents and sisters, I love you and appreciate all that you have done for me. Hopefully we can discuss this book someday.

Finally, Jessica. This is for you. You were there, every single day, knowing exactly what I needed to persevere. You are my favorite Crit. And now we have this little book to read to Frederick (when he's ready).

CONTENTS

CHAPTER 1

Moving Beyond Conservative Capture

Abstract This opening chapter introduces the reader to the core institution discussed within the book—the American law school—and reviews the current political science literature on the legal academy since the 1980s. This chapter details how the leading literature has been "captured by conservatism" and then explains why an investigation into the critical legal studies (CLS) movement will improve our understanding of the politics of the legal academy.

Keywords Law schools · Law professors · Conservatism · Critical legal studies

At the center of the American legal system lies the law school. As of this year, there are 199 law schools in the United States that are accredited by the American Bar Association and are approved to confer J.D. degrees.[1] This sizable legal academy educates scores of students and employs thousands of legal scholars. The most recent data shows that there are 9,494 full-time law professors that work at accredited law schools.[2]

But what do we know about American law schools? Until quite recently, there had been no thorough investigations of law schools or law professors as key players in American politics. Political scientists tended to

© The Author(s), under exclusive license to Springer Nature   1
Switzerland AG 2021
P. Baumgardner, *Critical Legal Studies*
and the Campaign for American Law Schools,
https://doi.org/10.1007/978-3-030-82378-8_1

look at the federal judiciary and other governmental institutions in order to gauge new directions in the law. Why waste time tracing the scholastic squabbles brewing in classrooms and across the pages of specialty journals when you can study the "real legal world" of judges, lawmakers, and other state actors? For generations, political scientists gave short shrift to law schools and those working within them.[3] In many years, one could have flipped through hundreds of pages of new research within leading political science journals without finding information on our nation's legal academy, legal scholars, legal movements, or legal scholarship.

Even those political scientists who specialized in the study of public law commonly ignored the value of law schools and law professors. One possible cause for this lack of attention is a Dahlian tradition that flourished within the public law subfield, which focused on law's role in American regimes and in political development almost exclusively through research into state and federal judiciaries.[4] Additionally, the state of judicial behavior research suggested a general lack of interest in how law schools, legal scholars, and legal scholarship shape the legal controversies before the courts, the legal professionals before the courts, and the legal reasoning used on the courts.[5]

And although political scientists have long appreciated the importance of intellectuals to political processes and to the study of American politics, the profound academic divide that existed between the domain of political science and the domain of law left certain key intellectuals understudied and underappreciated. Gerald Rosenberg, who spent decades straddling these two domains, explained:

> The academic disciplines of law and political science were once closely entwined under the rubric of the study of government. At the start of the twentieth century, to study government was to study law. The leading journals in each discipline published articles that were of mutual interest. Indeed, starting in 1910 the *American Political Science Review* published an annual doctrinal review of Supreme Court cases. In 1910 the review was written by Harvard Law Professor Eugene Wambaugh. He was followed by Thomas Reed Powell and then by political scientist Edward Corwin. The reviews continued until 1961. But as the century developed, and particularly after midcentury, the distance between the two disciplines grew. Today, legal academics and political scientists inhabit different worlds with little in common.[6]

With broad differences in training, professional development, modes of scholarship, civic influence, and relations to the modern research university, the academic disciplines of political science and law simply drifted apart. Although a handful of political scientists reached out to reconnect legal scholarship with political science scholarship, establish common rules for empirical research, and outline how best to influence public policy and judges' decision-making, these overtures represented outliers as the legal discipline remained a black box for many political scientists.[7]

Fortunately, in recent years some political scientists have begun to set their sights on the legal academy. These scholars recognize that overlooking this pivotal institution creates a troubling gap in the study of American politics, for the professional training, personnel, and intellectual currents in the law schools hold great influence over the future of American laws and the legal profession. Losing sight of the legal academy means losing sight of the powerful revolving door effects of the legal academy in the United States. Law schools not only produce our core legal professionals, but these institutions also mold a significant number of our nation's leading political players and fill a disproportionate number of government posts. As of 2018, 38% of US Representatives had earned a law degree, 55% of US Senators held JDs, and 15 of the 50 state governors had gone through law school. Of the ten individuals who have served as President of the United States over the past 50 years, five have held law degrees.[8]

Moreover, law professors maintain close ties to judges and administrative officials, and leading legal scholars also frequently become judges and administrative officials. Additionally, law schools provide law clerks to judges, movement lawyers to social causes, and—in full completion of the revolving door—they supply the next generation of law professors. As political scientists Amanda Hollis-Brusky and Joshua C. Wilson noted in their recent book, *Separate but Faithful: The Christian Right's Radical Struggle to Transform Law & Legal Culture*, law schools serve as indispensable sources of capital development in the United States "by attracting, creating, and credentialing professionals (*human capital*); establishing or being tied to networks for group advancement (*social capital*); and creating, spreading, and legitimating ideas within the legal, political, and wider publics (*intellectual* and *cultural capital*)."[9]

Put simply, law schools have an outsized role in the making of American public policy and in the crafting of our legal codes, and legal academics do profoundly shape the hearts and minds of future legal professionals. Ralph Nader was absolutely right when he declared: "Anyone who wishes to understand the legal crises that envelop the contemporary scene—in the cities, in the environment, in the courts, in the marketplace, in public services, in the corporate-government arenas and in Washington—should come to grips with this legal flow chart that begins with the law schools."[10]

Conservative Capture

Although it is a positive sign that a growing number of political scientists are beginning to appreciate—and research—the legal academy, troubling patterns have emerged within this new field of inquiry. In particular, the scholarship on American law schools and law professors has been unduly "captured by conservatism." Unquestionably, the dominant object of attention among political scientists who have begun researching the American legal academy has centered around the academy's relationship to the modern conservative legal movement and the role that law schools and legal scholars have played in supporting right-leaning developments in American law and politics since the 1980s.[11]

These accounts have been captured by conservatism in at least one of two senses. One form of conservative capture can be understood as conservative totalization. Many political science accounts conceptualize the major institutional and ideological developments—and also the failed developments—that have occurred in the legal academy over the past forty years strictly in terms of conservatization and the predictable result of various right-wing reform efforts. This form of conservative capture includes political science research that engages with the goings-on in the law schools for the sole purpose of highlighting the work of conservatives inside the academy (e.g., Federalist Society professors assisting or amplifying broader rightward reforms that have taken place in the United States since 1980) and research that delves into the law schools for the sole purpose of revealing the influence of outside conservatives on the academy (e.g., Republican politicians' decisions and conservative movement lawyering reshaping how the law is taught in the academy).

To find another example of conservative totalization, just look at the conventional commentary around the modern conservative legal movement. A common way of analyzing the conservative laws, policies, and political reforms that took place beginning in the 1980s requires us to view a nebulous umbrella collectivity—the modern conservative legal movement—as orchestrating one large-scale retrenchment project across the United States. The retrenchment efforts that we now associate with the "Reagan Revolution" were so seismic, this conventional analysis asserts, because they represented a singular challenge to the "form of elite, regime-enforcing professional knowledge" that had dominated the American legal system for decades.[12] "When it came to the courts and their intimate associates in legal academia and the broader legal culture, legal liberals called the tune" for much of the twentieth century.[13] But by the late 1970s and early 1980s, a new zeitgeist was emerging. A fragmented and aging band of legal liberals attempted to protect the achievements of the New Deal, the Great Society, and the Warren Court, while also safeguarding a particular vision of law's corrective power in American society. But this meager defense of the status quo proved futile as the Reaganites successfully uprooted decades of liberal state expansions and jurisprudential gains.[14] Accordingly, a good deal of the political science scholarship that has taken stock of the legal academy since the 1980s has focused primarily on the conservative legal movement's monumental retrenchment project, exploring how conservatives inside the legal academy advanced this retrenchment project and also how outside conservatives who were participating in this project came to influence the academy.

A second form of conservative capture that has taken place in political science research assigns a left fatalism to the American legal academy. In their investigations of law schools, political scientists have disregarded left-of-liberal reform efforts since the 1980s, thereby projecting a fatalism onto leftist reform. Little to no reference has been made to political attempts at socialist, communist, anarchist, or any other leftist reform in the legal academy, ostensibly because there have been no relevant leftist reform groups in the American law schools since the 1980s. It is easy to see how this form of conservative capture operates alongside conservative totalization; interpreting the main institutional and ideological developments that have occurred in the legal academy in terms of conservatization is quite natural when all manifestations of leftism have been pushed aside.

Of course, there are good reasons why contemporary researchers have emphasized the presence of conservatism within the American legal academy. Many political scientists have returned to the 1980s, in particular, for clues and context concerning the present day, oftentimes with the hope of deriving insights that can be wielded against the political agenda of the modern Right. Over the past few years, numerous academics have turned to news outlets and to the pages of professional journals to register their rage and revulsion toward President Donald Trump and the Republican Party. Understandably, one common feature of many professorial engagements with the modern Right has been a historical attempt to locate different actors within the multifarious networks and intellectual maps of the modern Right. Such an exercise is difficult to conclude without reference to the Reagan Revolution and the conservative developments in American law and politics that occurred during the 1980s.[15]

Regularly returning to the Reagan Revolution certainly is valuable for academics and non-academics alike. These sorts of remembrances and reappraisals bring attention to the core ideas and political strategies associated with the modern Right, thus equipping the present generation with a working knowledge of the basic *how* and *why* of recurring conservative mobilizations. For those who seek to retrench conservative laws and policies in the twenty-first century, returning to the 1980s also can identify possible cooptations of key tools and social movement resources from the past. Unfortunately, even though political scientists are returning to the 1980s for historical clarity and contemporary aid, many of the most theoretically rich and vocal legal reformers from the period have been overlooked.[16]

THE CRITICAL LEGAL STUDIES MOVEMENT

To date, political scientists have put forward a single narrative about the kind of critical juncture facing the American legal academy during the 1980s. This narrative dwells on the growth and empowerment of the conservative legal movement and holds up political conservatives as the only relevant actors engaged in sweeping, national attempts to attack elite law schools and to challenge the liberal consensus found within the legal academy. But this narrative loses sight of a separate revolutionary threat that existed within American law schools throughout the 1980s.

As a result of conservative capture, political scientists have completely ignored one of the most important reform movements operating across the legal academy during the 1980s. Lost in the sea of recent scholarship on the politics of the legal academy is the critical legal studies (CLS) movement. In fact, there is no serious political science research on the CLS movement, individual "Crits," or their leftist reforms of American law schools and the legal profession. This absence represents a major over-sight, for the CLS movement was a towering presence in the 1980s. The Crits' bid to fracture the academy's liberal consensus and to reform key elements of legal education was responsible for much of the academic soul-searching, political drama, and institutional development that took place throughout the decade. By the end of the 1980s, the Crits had left an indelible imprint on the American legal academy.

The pages ahead will track the rise and fall of the CLS movement across the 1980s. Originating from a small conference of legal radicals and New Leftist law professors, the CLS movement rapidly grew across the country, gained influence within law schools, and sought to advance its revolutionary agenda throughout the 1980s. This formidable left-wing movement sought to fundamentally reconstruct law schools, train a new generation of leftist lawyers, and replace the dominant form of legal consciousness governing the American legal system.

In addition to recovering the influential reform projects of the Crits, the chapters ahead highlight the strong academic and extra-academic reaction that developed against CLS. The movement was wildly successful during the first half of the 1980s, and Crits' leftist retrenchment efforts started to catch fire across the United States. But as the Crits' campaign for American law schools expanded, reactionary campaigns bent on curbing the red menace arose in the academy. Convinced that the CLS movement possessed a legal agenda that was too unprofessional and radical for new lawyers, a large group of professors, administrators, law school alumni, and concerned citizens mobilized during the second half of the 1980s to slow the Crits' momentum.

WHY CHRONICLE THE CRITS?

This is the first book within the discipline to chart the development of the CLS movement. While previous works have minimized the possi-bility of leftist legal development during the 1980s and have ignored the consequential struggles between ideologically diverse reformers from this period, this book spotlights the historic political activism of the CLS movement and demonstrates how the Crits' campaign for American law schools produced a dialectical professional environment and a series of political confrontations that profoundly shaped modern legal education.

This book is intended to correct academics' casual erasure of leftist reform from the legal transformations of the 1980s. Political scientists, in particular, have subsumed legal academic developments under the banner of conservative reform and have become preoccupied holding up the power and fait accompli of conservative reform during the 1980s. Consequently, the political science discipline has ignored real leftist reform efforts from the period and sidelined the remarkable movement dialectics that developed in the 1980s between leftist reformers and their reactionary opponents. This book places the CLS movement at the center of the 1980s legal academy and explores how the Crits' legacy continues to hold out political possibilities and reform lessons for leftist legal scholars today.

Instead of projecting a fatalism onto leftist reform, this book relies on extensive archival research and interviews to illuminate the radical potential that lived in the American legal academy of the 1980s. By foregrounding leftist scholars and political agendas that were ascendant and influential during the supposed apex of conservative legal reform in the United States, the following chapters approach a time period—the 1980s—and an institution—the law school—from a perspective that is at odds with conventional political science accounts.

NOTES

1. American Bar Association, "ABA-Approved Law Schools," https://www.americanbar.org/groups/legal_education/resources/aba_approved_law_schools/.
2. Stephanie Francis Ward, "How Many Tenured Law Professors Are Black? Public Data Does Not Say," *ABA Journal*, October 28, 2020. https://www.abajournal.com/web/article/how-many-tenured-law-professors-are-black-public-data-does-not-say#:~:text=For%20the%202019%20reports%2C%20there,of%20whom%20identified%20as%20minorities.
3. For more on this disciplinary problem, see Paul Baumgardner, "'Something He and His People Naturally Would Be Drawn To': The Reagan Administration and the Law-and-Economics Movement," *Presidential Studies Quarterly*, Vol. 49 (2019).
4. Robert Dahl, "Decision-Making in a Democracy: The Supreme Court as National Policy Maker," *Journal of Public Law*, Vol. 6 (1957).
5. See, e.g., Jeffrey A. Segal and Harold J. Spaeth, *The Supreme Court and the Attitudinal Model Revisited* (New York, NY: Cambridge University Press, 2002); Michael A. Bailey and Forrest Maltzman, *The Constrained Court: Law, Politics, and the Decisions Justices Make* (Princeton: Princeton University Press, 2011); Jeffrey R. Lax and Charles M. Cameron, "Bargaining and Opinion Assignment on the US Supreme Court," *Journal of*

Law, Economics, and Organization, Vol. 23, No. 2 (2007); Chad Westerland, Jeffrey A. Segal, Lee Epstein, Charles M. Cameron and Scott Comparato, "Strategic Defiance and Compliance in the U.S. Courts of Appeals," *American Journal of Political Science*, Vol. 54, No. 4 (2010).

6. Gerald N. Rosenberg, "Across the Great Divide (Between Law and Political Science)," *Green Bag*, Vol. 3, No. 3 (2000): 267.

7. Ibid.; Lee Epstein and Gary King, "The Rules of Inference," *University of Chicago Law Review*, Vol. 69, No. 1 (2002); Robert J. Spitzer, *Saving the Constitution from Lawyers: How Legal Training and Law Reviews Distort Constitutional Meaning* (Cambridge, UK and New York: Cambridge University Press, 2008).

8. Congressional Research Service, "Membership of the 115th Congress: A Profile," *CRS Report R44762*. December 20, 2018. https://fas.org/sgp/crs/misc/R44762.pdf; Center on the American Governor, "Fast Facts about American Governors," Rutgers University, May 2019. http://governors.rutgers.edu/on-governors/us-governors/fast-facts-about-american-governors/; Sahil Chinoy and Jessica Ma, "How Every Member Got to Congress," *New York Times*, January 26, 2019. https://www.nytimes.com/interactive/2019/01/26/opinion/sunday/paths-to-congress.html.

9. Amanda Hollis-Brusky and Joshua C. Wilson, *Separate but Faithful: The Christian Right's Radical Struggle to Transform Law & Legal Culture* (New York: Oxford University Press, 2020): 15.

10. Ralph Nader, "Law Schools and Law Firms," *University of Minnesota Law Review*, Vol. 54, No. 3 (1970): 494.

11. See, e.g., Simon Zschirnt, *Legal Intellectual Movements in Political Time: Reconstructive Leadership and Transformations of Legal Thought and Discourse* (El Paso, TX: LFB Scholarly Publishing, 2015); Laura Hatcher, "Economic Libertarians, Property and Institutions: Linking Activism, Ideas, and Identities among Property Rights Advocates," in *The Worlds Cause Lawyers Make: Structure and Agency in Legal Practice*, eds. Austin Sarat and Stuart A. Scheingold (Stanford, CA: Stanford University Press, 2005); Jefferson Decker, *The Other Rights Revolution: Conservative Lawyers and the Remaking of American Government* (New York: Oxford University Press, 2016); Steven M. Teles, *The Rise of the Conservative Legal Movement: The Battle for Control of the Law* (Princeton, NJ: Princeton University Press: 2008); Daniel Bennett, *Defending Faith: The Politics of the Christian Conservative Legal Movement* (Lawrence, KS: University Press of Kansas, 2017); Joshua C. Wilson and Amanda Hollis-Brusky, "Higher Law: Can Christian Conservatives Transform Law Through Legal Education?" *Law & Society Review*, Vol. 52, No. 4 (2018); Hollis-Brusky and Wilson (2020); Thomas M. Keck, *The Most Activist Supreme Court in History: The Road to Modern Judicial Conservatism*

(Chicago & London: University of Chicago Press, 2004); Ken I. Kersch, *Conservatives and the Constitution: Imagining Constitutional Restoration in the Heyday of American Liberalism* (New York: Cambridge University Press, 2019); Elliott Ash, Daniel L. Chen, and Suresh Naidu, "Ideas Have Consequences: The Impact of Law and Economics on American Justice," Unpublished manuscript (2019); Calvin TerBeek, "'Clocks Must Always Be Turned Back': *Brown v. Board of Education* and the Racial Origins of Constitutional Originalism," *American Political Science Review* (forthcoming).

12. Kersch (2019), 362.
13. Ibid.
14. See Teles (2008) and Kersch (2019).
15. Paul Baumgardner, "Ronald Reagan, The Modern Right, and...the Rise of the Fem-Crits," *Laws*, Vol. 8, No. 4 (2019).
16. Ibid.

CHAPTER 2

The Birth of the CLS Movement

Abstract This chapter explores the origins of the CLS movement. The Crits emerged during the late 1970s under a specific set of political and educational circumstances. And although the overwhelming majority of Crits were legal scholars, they did not become a school of thought or the wing of a mass movement. Instead, the Crits elected to organize a legal movement.

Keywords Critical legal studies · Law schools · Law professors · Legal movements · Liberalism

Within the political science discipline, several scholars have begun researching the modern American legal academy, with special attention paid to the political influence of law schools since 1980. Unfortunately, the consequential history of the critical legal studies (CLS) movement has been left out of this emerging scholarship on the politics of the legal academy. Although the CLS movement was a substantial political force in American law schools during the 1980s, political science research generally only focuses on two groupings during this period: fading liberal

© The Author(s), under exclusive license to Springer Nature
Switzerland AG 2021
P. Baumgardner, *Critical Legal Studies
and the Campaign for American Law Schools,*
https://doi.org/10.1007/978-3-030-82378-8_2

consensus forces and burgeoning conservative forces. The CLS movement simply flies under the radar, while conservative forces such as the
law-and-economics movement take center stage.

In the case of law-and-economics, the common historical telling goes
something like this: a group of neoclassical law professors—many of them
trained at, or teaching at, the University of Chicago—served as natural
allies of political conservatism and fortuitously emerged and ascended
in the 1980s. The academy was a riper and easier place for conservative development than expected. The "lawyer-economists" good ideas
blossomed in a favorable political climate, clearing the way for further
conservative legal scholars to thrive. On the open canvas of law school
life, incisive conservative ideas gained traction on their own. All it took
was a few conferences, friendships, savvy networking, and *voila*, law-and-
economics became entrenched. There is no story here—just an old guard
of law professors and academic practices becoming passé and conservative
forces such as the law-and-economics movement being birthed into prestige and intellectual status. The academic front for the rise of the legal
conservatism was set fairly easily, so little time is spent explaining it.[1]

But it is vitally important that political scientists working on the politics
of the legal academy do not forget about the CLS movement. Organizing
and operating within the law schools during the 1980s, this group of
leftist legal scholars struggled to radically reorient American law. These
academics intentionally and purposively engaged in political action—tied
to their scholarly work—which extended to legal professionals across the
United States. And the Crits' political action did not go unnoticed. In
fact, the CLS movement generated a remarkable series of shocks, institutional responses, and retaliations during the 1980s, which would impact
the future course of the American legal academy.

Before delving into the movement's legacy in the legal academy, this
chapter explores how CLS began. The pages ahead return us to the little
known beginnings of the CLS movement, explaining both the origin of
the movement and the type of collectivity that the Crits formed in the
late 1970s. I hope to make clear in this chapter that although CLS was
heterodox in many ways, the movement stands as a valuable source of
political research. The Crits would come to stimulate powerful reactions
from legal professionals in the United States, and a diverse cast of char-
acters both inside and outside of the law schools would have to swoop
in to stymie the movement's ideas and retrenchment efforts. For a threat
so severe that law school alums and private organizations were willing to

dedicate their time and money to curb the red scare, and for a collectivity so "booming" that hundreds of academic and popular articles were written to address CLS claims,[2] and for a movement so menacing that law schools were forced to exploit hiring and firing processes, teaching protocols, and faculty incentives in order to contain it, it is high time that political scientists take a closer look at the Crits.

MAKING THE MOVEMENT: ORIGINS, TIMING, AND COLLECTIVE FORMATION

Up to this point, no political scientist has provided a proper evaluation of the key organizational dimensions of CLS or has tried to explain the type of political collectivity that CLS represented. In this chapter and the next, we will uncover the ways in which Crits understood themselves collectively—as a collectivity—within the American legal academy, focusing on the ways in which these legal scholars approached the theoretical and practical projects of the CLS movement within their political environments. By carefully illustrating the movement's identity, these chapters offer major insights into the particular ideas, strategies, forms of mobilization, and locations of conflict that defined the politics of the Crits.

"The Situation"

To understand the origin of critical legal studies, some Sartre is essential—meaning existence precedes essence. So here there is a relatively intuitive, untheorized but very powerful intuition about one's existential situation, which is one is miserable in the political, emotional, professional environment that one finds one in for reasons that are vaguely left. That's "the situation." And then the natural thing to do, especially for people like this, is to theorize the situation, to address it practically. Theorizing and addressing it practically are not the same thing as being in the situation, and the basis of the group is being in the situation. Then, within the situation, people set out to theorize, instrumentalize, pragmatize, work out ideas about why it's wrong and what to do about it, but also about what to do in the organization.[3]

In *The Rise of the Conservative Legal Movement*, Steven Teles observed that the social movement literature largely understands mobilization either in terms of political opportunity or resource mobilization.[4] Teles rightly noted how "[b]oth of these theories...assume that organization is an automatic, agentless response either to opportunity or to resources. A useful theory of social movement organization needs to pry open this black box of organizational development, to explain where effective organizations come from and how their leaders use them."[5] In order to study the politically conservative forces that began organizing in the 1970s, Teles was interested in first "situating political agents in an inherited regime that sets the conditions under which strategic decisions are made."[6] To fully understand the Crits, a similar line of inquiry is required. The building of a movement in the late 1970s and 1980s out of American legal scholars, in general, and culled from a geographically dispersed set of radical leftist legal academics, in particular, was quite a feat—a feat that is rendered intelligible through an acute understanding of American law and politics during this period.

Much like conservatives, leftist law professors and law students in the late 1970s experienced a sense of intellectual "isolation" and professional alienation surrounding their place and purpose in the American legal system.[7] In an attempt to bring together likeminded individuals and provide "an opportunity for the kind of intellectual exchange that would help us become a critical community," a group of left-wing legal scholars hosted the first Conference on Critical Legal Studies (CCLS) at the University of Wisconsin-Madison in 1977.[8] This first CCLS served as the organizational foundation for the critical legal studies movement.

But before approaching the creation of the CCLS, we should unpack the origins of disillusionment, isolation, alienation, and mutual criticality that served, first, as the catalyst for connecting leftist academics who were spread across the country and then, later on, as the existential core for the CLS movement. A central alienating force for many leftist legal scholars during this period was what they perceived to be the entrenched interests and ideologies of the American legal academy. Most commonly, this bugbear was attacked as a docile, don't-rock-the-boat liberalism. As Duncan Kennedy—a central figure in CLS—notes, a significant number of radical legal scholars believed:

[T]he liberal elites who dominate both government and academia across all domains of knowledge had over a period of time (that might vary, but certainty since 1960) pursued disastrous, wrong, bad policies and that the dominant liberal elites understood intelligent thinking about society, law, and politics to lead to the conclusion that radical breaks with the status quo were not feasible and/or not desirable.[9]

Equally concerning for professors like Kennedy was the fact that the American Left appeared listless, fractured, and utterly de-radicalized. Crits believed that they had a big part to play in questioning the legally sanctioned inequality existing in the United States and stopping the nation's "blind lurching between protracted stagnation and rare and risky revolution."[10] But an impression deepened among the legal scholars who would form the core of CLS that liberal attempts to produce social change merely through the protection of individual rights was not the best strategy for moving to a more just and democratic legal order. A new piece of legislation, a positive court decision, or even the next electoral victory would not immediately produce radical egalitarian legal reforms.[11]

The Warren Court was over and its liberal legacy fading under the Burger Court. The Left could not quickly and effectively halt the years of bloodshed in Vietnam. Labor unions were beginning to crumble, and the national face of the Democratic Party was a moderate and mild-mannered Southern Baptist. Moreover, a significant number of radical legal scholars observed the Democratic plans to address the unjust hierarchies of class, race, and gender encoded in American law as either weak or oddly content with a tact of gradual reformism—process and propriety being privileged over meaningful, aggressive efforts to generate long-term structural changes. Critical legal scholar Robert Gordon recalls how these generational dynamics worked to bring leftist legal scholars together in opposition to the dominant ideology of their elders: "We were criticizing what we saw as the complacency of this form of liberalism, and it was very complacent. It basically claimed to have solved the problems of class violence and class conflict and racial exclusion and illegitimate subordination and hierarchy in American life. So a lot of the critique was directed against that claim."[12]

The Crits were particularly interested in diagnosing and treating the listlessness that pervaded the American legal academy. "When we came, they were like a priesthood that had lost their faith and kept their jobs. They stood in tedious embarrassment before cold altars. But we turned away from those altars and found the mind's opportunity in the heart's revenge," one Crit wrote about the previous generation of legal academics.[13] Although many elite American law professors during this period were politically liberal, these liberals were of a staid variety. Many young Crit professors viewed their older colleagues as doing little to remedy the problems facing American legal institutions and practices. Instead, complacency, docility, and political passivity had become the norm within the legal academy. Association of American Law School meetings embodied professional detachment and inaction, as "speakers...simply mouth[ed] off piously, making themselves and the liberals in the audience feel good" but then pooh-poohed any ideas to act. These professors had created a professional environment in which "the political vision, the political will and even the political skills to <u>do</u> anything about the responsibility of legal education for our unjust society" were nonexistent.[14]

Instead, the "cosy liberal consensus" that existed in many elite law schools promoted the view "that the system is basically OK."[15] For example, the legal process tradition continued to hold considerable weight in many American law schools. Within this tradition, law students were trained to see the American legal system as natural, rule-guided, and coherent. In the classroom, students were instructed to "think like a lawyer," which often merely entailed a blind identification with the judge or the client on any given legal matter.[16] Legal reasoning was taught as a technical practice of weighing legitimate interests, uncovering germane principles, and appropriately sorting this-or-that policy matter into sharply defined institutional spaces governed by historically refined rules.[17] Such a complacent liberal approach weighed on the Crits. In Duncan Kennedy's *Legal Education and the Reproduction of Hierarchy: A Polemic Against the System*—a book humorously described as the Little Red Book of the CLS movement—Kennedy encapsulated this formative charge of the early Crits. Kennedy dissected the multiple ways in which the archetypal, elite American law school's "errors have a bias in favor of the center-liberal program of limited reform of the market economy and pro forma gestures toward racial and sexual equality." According to Kennedy, "The bias arises because law school teaching makes the choice of hierarchy and domination, which is implicit in the adoption of the rules of property, contract and tort, look as though it flows from legal reasoning, rather than from politics and economics."[18]

So when Mark Tushnet sent out an announcement for the first CCLS in 1977, he and the Organizing Committee of Richard Abel, Tom Heller, Morton Horwitz, Duncan Kennedy, Stewart Macaulay, Rand Rosenblatt, David Trubek, and Roberto Unger were trying to gather a group of leftist legal academics with a shared "negative reaction to a situation."[19] The

negativity toward the American legal academy and the broader legal liberalism of the American legal system was the basis for the CLS movement
and its organizational foundation, the CCLS. "This is the type of group
that is organized initially around a rejection, an experience of alienation
and antagonism towards a situation that you're in," Kennedy has reiterated.[20] Crits were organized around their mutual sense of alienation,
powerlessness, intellectual anxiety, and the disconnect they felt between
their own radical identities and the American legal academy. The CLS
movement was intended to somehow overcome this malaise, by charting
out an authentic and purposeful leftist identity in law and crafting a
community that would politically engage together.

Settling on a Collective Identity

By design, the majority of those invited to the first CCLS in 1977
were leftist law professors and radical lawyers—not mainstream liberals
and certainly not conservatives. As the Crit John Henry Schlegel fondly
recalls, the dean of Yale Law School "first protested that members of
his faculty, obviously as smart and as 'with it' as any around, were
being excluded for no good reason. He then retreated wholly satisfied,
upon being informed that the criterion for extending invitations was not
smarts but politics and that on this criterion the Yale faculty was not left
enough."[21]

As David Trubek, one of the founders of CLS[22] wrote afterward,
the first CCLS was "an act of hope" and also an "act of reconstruction" for many of these leftists.[23] The founding members of CLS had
witnessed the faltering of New Left movements in recent years, and they
intended to somehow "overcome the disadvantages that caused New Left
movements to fail."[24] At the first CCLS, there was an explicit focus on
community building, instead of theoretical bickering, power brokering,
and immediate fractionalization.[25]

It was clear that this group shared a particular kind of leftist political
orientation. These were radicals held together by a common criticality
toward the legal system in the United States, the dominant ideas,
personnel, and structural powers within the law schools, and the growing
conservative forces in American society. Crits were New Leftist, radical
egalitarian, legal scholars who looked at other (generally older) legal
scholars and were "repelled by their sterility and thorough disconnection
from actual social life" and the problems of mainstream American law.[26]

Kennedy aptly described this sort of legal radical in *Legal Education and the Reproduction of Hierarchy*:

> What makes one a radical, in this view, is not that one is against hierarchy, since we all sometimes accept it, nor that one is against 'illegitimate' hierarchy, since we're all against that. Nor is the radical the person with the theory that 'goes to the root.' None of us has such a theory. The radical is the person who <u>wants to go further</u>, right now, practically, to dismantle existing structures of hierarchy that look evil, and <u>wants to go further</u>, right now, practically, in confronting or subverting the forces that keep them in place.[27]

Following the first CCLS, Crits began the herculean labor of constructing a leftist community. Members started discussing the CLS organizational structure, political mission, finances, future events, committee responsibilities, and avenues of faculty recruitment and support.[28] But what shape would this collection of legal radicals take? Seeing the faces of fellow travelers and commiserating about the unfavorable legal system around you is good and well, but what would be the purpose of a critical legal studies movement? Did it even have to be a movement? One Crit, David Trubek, beautifully captured both the element of freedom and uncertainty that reigned at the first CCLS in 1977: "It is almost as if we had been picked up from our familiar surroundings and deposited in a new and strange terrain. Now we must develop new bearings so that we can grasp the new geography."[29]

As CLS started to gain its footing, develop diverse movement events, and expand its membership, it would settle on a specific collective identity. At first, the young group looked like it could go down one of three paths: CLS could organize into the wing of a mass movement, it could become a school of thought, or the Crits could build their own legal movement.

Mass Movement Wing

As previously discussed, the CLS movement is given short shrift among American political scientists and political science departments. If any work related to critical legal studies is assigned in a public law or jurisprudence course, it is generally one work: legal philosopher Roberto Mangabeira Unger's *The Critical Legal Studies Movement*.[30] For some reason, Unger's text remains the go-to work when academics want to quickly characterize and caricature critical legal scholarship and the CLS movement. However, although readers may turn to "the most influential, philosophically adept, and historically and sociologically learned exponent of the Movement" for the *CliffsNotes* on CLS, some of Unger's aspirations for and assessments of the movement are idiosyncratic—a fact that even he concedes.[31] The central reason for these idiosyncrasies is the fact that Unger wanted CLS to orient itself toward the capture of state power, by morphing into the legal wing of a larger leftist movement. In this role, CLS could provide legal ideas and resources for progressive reformers bent on radicalizing both the bar and American government.

Unger's original and ill-fated plan is first sketched out in an ambitious "after-dinner speech, delivered at the Sixth Annual Conference in Critical Legal Studies" in March 1982.[32] The speech was then published in the *Harvard Law Review* in 1983 and later turned into the canonical book, *The Critical Legal Studies Movement*. But far from offering a realistic intellectual history or a careful retelling of the main programmatic features of the movement, Unger's speech/article/book represents one Crit's vision for CLS in the early years of the radical group.

One of the most influential legal philosophers of the late 1970s and also one of the nine members of the Organizing Committee for the first CCLS in 1977, Roberto Unger pushed the collectivity to become part of a mass movement, which would work to inform and guide on-the-ground political efforts aimed at broadscale social transformation throughout the United States. Unlike the schools of thought that were popping up in American law schools during the 1970s, Unger urged CLS to become a "movement" with an eye toward critique and reconstruction of the state.[33]

But the CLS movement self-consciously moved in a different direction than Unger proposed. As David Trubek remembers, "Roberto always believed in state power, believed that the purpose was to gain state power. But the fact was that CLS people weren't interested in state power—partly because they didn't think it was a real possibility."[34] Peter Gabel agrees: "It never occurred to us, I would say, certainly me, that we would be trying to engage in the type of funding and legitimation that the Federalist Society was seeking to do, because we were a movement-inspired force. I'm contrasting that with a force that seeks to impose institutional authority. That wasn't who we were."[35]

Although there were some members, in addition to Unger, who wanted CLS to become the legal wing of a mass movement, so that the Crits would be well positioned to gain influence within more formal political channels and legal processes, Trubek and many other Crits did not believe that this option represented the best path for CLS.[36] As such, the movement would craft a political agenda that did not include lobbying campaigns for legal reform, pushing trial cases through the courts, shaping ballot measures, facilitating members' ascent into government positions, or offering legal ideas, writings, or other forms of intellectual support to a mass movement. In short, the Crits did not engage in the same host of orthodox mass movement activities that many conservative forces executed throughout the 1980s.

Almost thirty years after the publication of *The Critical Legal Studies Movement*, Unger released an updated version of his classic text. In this most recent publication, titled *The Critical Legal Studies Movement: Another Time, A Greater Task*, Unger has two missions: (1) offer a renewed call to arms for the next generation of legal radicals and (2) vocalize criticisms and tremendous disappointment about the CLS movement. The latter becomes the more pronounced mission in *Another Time, A Greater Task*, as Unger returns to judge CLS against a backdrop of the road not taken—or, more specifically, *his* road not taken.

Unger is most scathing (and personal) on this point. Although CLS was on the right track and enjoyed a number of meaningful successes, Unger laments that the movement engaged in a "half-hearted prosecution" of the real political project at hand.[37] In the updated book's introduction, he poses the question: "For what did critical legal studies stand?"[38] Unger identifies separate strands of the leftist movement and gestures toward major figures in the movement, such as Duncan Kennedy and Morton Horwitz, who advanced them. Unfortunately, Unger claims, each of these strands handicapped CLS and bred projects crippled by intellectual and institutional weaknesses.

Unger then reveals a final strand of CLS, "the least remarked" yet "most novel" position: his own position, as articulated in his 1982 speech to the Conference on Critical Legal Studies and in *The Critical Legal Studies Movement*.[39] According to Unger, the movement had the potential to pursue an "institutionalist approach," by unearthing and exploiting the critical junctures in American politics and law and then supplying institutional alternatives.[40] But CLS lacked this essential "institutional program"; the Crits never produced or allied with a suitable "surrogate" to expand and implement their political work, as Unger sees the legal realists having done with the New Dealers in the 1930s.[41] If CLS had pursued this institutionalist approach and been part of a real mass movement, the Crits may have become larger players in American law and politics. Instead, the CLS movement "failed in its most important task" and left the United States in a moment of darkening.[42]

School of Thought

The second option that gained limited support within the nascent CLS movement was to organize into a school of thought.[43] Schools of thought usually are collectivities in the loosest of senses. They do not possess a high degree of formal organization, and they are constituted as collectivities predominantly via shared theoretical and disciplinary tools, methodologies, affinities, habits, viewpoints, and aims.

In this instance, a CLS school of thought would produce high-quality scholarship and establish a CLS research program for legal academics. And some Crits did think that critical legal studies should "stay put" and operate as a school of thought within the law schools, instead of dedicating time and attention to recruiting and organizing leftist legal scholars into a lasting political presence or engaging in sundry forms of political activism. Advocates for this form of collectivity thought that if the main function of CLS and its organizational foundation, the CCLS, was to craft a coherent research program, the movement would be able to trigger profound legal effects, even though the collectivity would be directed toward a fairly circumscribed and largely intellectual endeavor.

Part of the reason for this advocacy was the belief that legal education already was on the verge of becoming an overtly politicized professional environment. Of course, the American legal academy had always been a place of politics, for scholarship, pedagogy, course composition, faculty-student-administrative relations, university mission, (re)production of the bar, learning standards and expectations, newly minted lawyers' cultivated attitudes, placement expectations, and inter-institutional social status competitions—*Sorry, Yalie. Harvard Law actually is better!*—all possess political content and can readily become the root of significant political action. But, during the middle of the twentieth century, the extent to which these various materials were consciously contested and became the root of significant political action within American law schools was minimal.[44]

However, by the time that CLS was conceived, the legal academy's unobtrusive environment was opening to challenge.[45] American legal education was undergoing a remarkable change, a change that David Trubek refers to as the "academization" or "intellectualization of the law school."[46] This phenomenon seemed to create ample room for dissident legal academics, like the Crits:

> Left, right or center, law schools were very professional and oriented around professional issues and limited to professional discourse...At some point a change occurs. The first highly visible version of this was the Law and Society Association, which starts in '64. The law-and-economics movement comes along a little later as an organized activity, and there was a lot of money put into that project (and it wasn't to bring about the socialist revolution). But intellectual stuff was good. I used to say that you knew that something had changed when the word 'reification' appeared more frequently in the issue of the *Harvard Law Review* than the word 'jurisdiction'. This is important because it meant that there was space that didn't exist before. So all of a sudden there was this academic space, let's call it the academization. Law schools started looking more like social science departments and universities were encouraging it... This was a sea change in American law schools. CLS comes at a time when there's space for things that would have been very hard to accomplish [before].[47]

Some Crits—such as John H. Schlegel—viewed CLS as the proper vehicle for critiquing, subverting, and reconstructing the susceptible American legal academy. As legal academics newly ensconced in the law schools, Crits could do what academics do best: teach and write articles. This theory-building venture held out the promise of substantial legal impact, because Crit professors could engage their non-radical peers in professional journals, either persuading or outmaneuvering other scholars in the pages of law reviews. CLS meetings and other academic events would center around sharpening each other's ideas and writings, while building a definably CLS research program. However, although some members within the early CLS movement thought that a school of thought was the right way to go, and that any collective formation more grandiose than a school of thought would be the wrong direction for the movement, the Crits did not become a school of thought.[48]

Legal Movement

On the possibility of CLS morphing into the legal wing of a broader, mass movement, Robert Gordon remarks: "You know, I am by vocation a scholar and an intellectual...I was not made to lead mass popular movements."[49] As per the insulated, theory-building option afforded by a school of thought, Duncan Kennedy notes that almost "everybody thinks that it should be more than that."[50] So now that the porridge has been found to be too hot in one bowl and too cold in another, we come to the bowl that was just right for CLS.

It is clear from CCLS notes, correspondences between various Crits, the framing and agendas of CLS meetings, critical legal scholarship from the 1980s, and interviews with Crits that CLS became a legal movement constituted and led by legal scholars who were determined to bridge theory and praxis across a diverse range of legal fields. In the words of one Crit, the CLS movement "links its intellectual projects with the political and social aspiration of its membership."[51] This legal movement actively recruited, connected, and mobilized radical legal scholars who desired "to fuse theory and radical legal practice."[52] For instance, although recruitment was important to CLS, the movement remained geared toward scholars—primarily law professors and future law professors.[53] As another Crit explained, "Critical Legal Studies is basically a movement of legal intellectuals."[54] The CLS movement was interested in attracting jurists—those priests and prophets of the law who were endowed with ideals and "higher pretensions," and who were interested in "participating in the contest over the future of law and thus of society."[55]

Many Crits have emphasized the legal movement dimensions of CLS. Duncan Kennedy has claimed that "the basic CLS idea/organizational strategy" concerned the inseparable "combination of internal and external critique."[56] Reporting on a speech that Mark Tushnet gave about CLS in 1987, the editor of the *Ohio State* University Moritz College of *Law*'s *Law Record*, stressed how all strands of CLS "urge adherents to take political action."[57] For although Crits were deeply committed to their academic work, the CLS movement was just as deeply committed to political mobilization. According to one Crit, Gary Minda, the CLS movement constructed a political collectivity "focused on the 'doing' rather than just the 'theorizing.'"[58] These two practices—theorizing and doing—proved to be intimately connected within CLS. In the words of Robert Gordon: "Our intellectual perspective also leads to certain forms of political argument and political conclusions, and what's wrong with that?"[59]

Throughout the 1980s, CLS sought to support and connect these leftist scholars' work, extending it into various forms of political action. Writing to the "Critical Legal Studies Organizing Committee, Summer Campers, and other interested People" in 1982, Rand E. Rosenblatt discussed the upcoming CCLS and described the movement's "perennial interest" in manifesting members' scholarly work into different legal practices.[60] In this way, CLS became a sort of "practical policy generating method."[61] Instead of simply offering their services as intellectual entrepreneurs or handmaidens to a broader political collectivity, this legal movement of leftist law professors became involved in their own unique political actions.

One vocal Crit, Karl Klare, made this precise point when responding to Ed Sparer, a law professor at the University of Pennsylvania Law School, in January 1982. Klare wrote that he was "aggrieved" by Sparer's criticism that, in Klare's words, "the relationship between CLS and actual political struggle is minuscule, and that we are hardly influenced by social movement practice, let alone active in it."[62] Klare rejoined: "These claims are patently false and not a little bit insulting…if you were more familiar with the people involved in CLS you would hesitate to publish such claims." For one thing, CLS had become remarkably successful in organizing leftist legal scholars across the country: "it is striking how narrowly instrumental your notion of 'political organizing' is, so that you would apparently fail to credit as bona fide political work the organization of several hundred law teachers and lawyers into an increasingly vocal oppositional force within our profession." Moreover, Klare made clear, the fact that CLS was constituted and led by scholars did not militate against its movement identity:

> Your ideas about theory are based on a very narrow and traditional view of left politics, namely that the role of 'intellectuals' is restricted to helping other people; that we have no legitimate stake of our own in social transformation. This leads you to underestimate the importance of struggles within the academy and the professions and to overlook valuable opportunities for political confrontation.[63]

As we will see in the chapters ahead, the actions and movement strategies embraced by the Crits could strike their colleagues as both peculiar and incendiary. But Klare and others rejected the view that their actions and strategies were removed from "real politics." The Crits' "effort to link the study and practice of the law to the transformation of the society in which we live in a more egalitarian, democratic direction" was a very real and a very bold political ambition, an ambition which pushed hundreds of Crits to attack the racist, sexist, and capitalist foundations of the American legal system.[64]

NOTES

1. See, e.g., Neil Duxbury, *Patterns of American Jurisprudence* (New York: Oxford University Press, 1995); Laura Kalman, *The Strange Career of Legal Liberalism* (New Haven: Yale University Press, 1996); Hatcher (2005). Also see Baumgardner (2019a).
2. G. Edward White, "The Inevitability of Critical Legal Studies," *Stanford Law Review*, Vol. 36, No. 1–2 (1984): 649.
3. Duncan Kennedy, Interview with Author.
4. Teles (2008), 14.
5. Ibid., 15.
6. Ibid.
7. Baumgardner (2019b); Mark Tushnet, "Proposal for First Conference on Critical Legal Studies," January 17, 1977; Maurice J. Holland, "A Hurried Perspective on the Critical Legal Studies Movement: The Marx Brothers Assault The Citadel," *Harvard Journal of Law and Public Policy*, Vol. 8 (1985): 243.
8. Tushnet (1977); Duncan Kennedy, *Legal Education and the Reproduction of Hierarchy: A Polemic Against the System* (New York and London: New York University Press, 2004): 203–4.
9. Kennedy, Interview.
10. Roberto Mangabeira Unger, *The Critical Legal Studies Movement* (Cambridge, MA and London: Harvard University Press, 1986): 93.
11. See, e.g., Duncan Kennedy, "The Critique of Rights in Critical Legal Studies," in *Left Legalism/Left Critique*, eds. Wendy Brown and Janet Halley (Durham, NC and London: Duke University Press, 2002); Mark Tushnet, "The Critique of Rights," *SMU Law Review*, Vol. 47, No. 1 (1994); Mark Tushnet, "Essay on Rights," *Texas Law Review*, Vol. 62, No. 8 (1984); Guyora Binder, "On Critical Legal Studies as Guerrilla Warfare," *Georgetown Law Journal*, Vol. 76, No. 1 (1987); Peter Gabel and Duncan Kennedy, "Roll Over Beethoven," *Stanford Law Review*, Vol. 36, No. 1–2 (1984).
12. Robert Gordon, Interview with Author.

13. Roberto Mangabeira Unger, "The Critical Legal Studies Movement," *Harvard Law Review*, Vol. 96, No. 3 (1983): 675.
14. Baumgardner (2019b) and Duncan Kennedy, ed., "News of the AALS," *Lizard*, No. 1, San Francisco, CA, January 5, 1984: 1–2.
15. Kennedy (2004), 37–38.
16. I am thankful to Jeremy Paul for offering this important insight.
17. CLS descriptions of the problematic legal process tradition abound. See, e.g., Robert W. Gordon, "American Law Through English Eyes: A Century of Nightmares and Noble Dreams," *Georgetown Law Journal*, Vol. 84 (1996); Gary Minda, "The Jurisprudential Movements of the 1980s," *Ohio State Law Journal*, Vol. 50, No. 3 (1989); John Henry Schlegel, "Notes Toward an Intimate, Opinionated, and Affectionate History of the Conference on Critical Legal Studies," *Stanford Law Review*, Vol. 36, No. 1–2 (1984); Duncan Kennedy, "Left Theory and Left Practice: A Memoir in the Form of a Speech," *Transnational Legal Theory*, Vol. 5, No. 4 (2014).
18. Baumgardner (2019b) and Kennedy (2004), 37.
19. Kennedy, Interview.
20. Ibid.
21. Schlegel (1984), 399–400.
22. On Trubek and Kennedy being at the core of the early CLS movement, see ibid., 392–95.
23. David M. Trubek, "Slaying Dragons or Creating Them? Preliminary Reactions to the First Conference on Critical Legal Studies," *Conference on Critical Legal Studies Newsletter*, No. 1, June 6, 1977: 1.
24. Kennedy, Interview.
25. Schlegel (1984), 399.
26. Mark Kelman, *A Guide to Critical Legal Studies* (London and Cambridge, MA: Harvard University Press, 1987): 1; Adam Gearey, "'Change is Gonna Come': Critical Legal Studies and the Legacies of the New Left," *Law and Critique*, Vol. 24, No. 3 (2013); Peter Gabel and Paul Harris, "Building Power and Breaking Images: Critical Legal Theory and the Practice of Law," *New York University Review of Law & Social Change*, Vol. 11, No. 3 (1983); "Key Ideas," *Critical Legal Studies: Intellectual History and the History of the Present*, February, 28, 2020, Princeton, NJ.
27. Kennedy (2004), 81. Adding a bit more substance to this description nearly fifteen years after the first CCLS, Karl Klare described the Crits' legal theoretical commitments "to democracy (to extending self-determination and participatory decisionmaking in 'politics' and in the 'private' spheres of work, family, and institutional life); to economic, social, racial, and gender equality; to ending poverty; to feminism and sexual pluralism; to multiculturalism; to saving the environment; to international economic equality; and to nonviolence in international affairs."

Karl E. Klare, "Discussion Document for Saturday Morning Plenary: Do the Critical Legal Theory Networks Have a Politics?" April 11, 1992: 1.

28. T. Heller, S. Macaulay, D. Trubek, and M. Tushnet, "Future Activities of the Conference," 1977.

29. Trubek (1977), 2.

30. Unger (1986).

31. J.M. Finnis, "On 'The Critical Legal Studies Movement'," *American Journal of Jurisprudence*, Vol. 30, No. 1 (1985): 22; Roberto Mangabeira Unger, *The Critical Legal Studies Movement: Another Time, a Greater Task* (London and New York: Verso, 2015).

32. Unger (2015), 42.

33. Ibid., 79, 91; Unger (1986), 25–42, 57.

34. David Trubek, Interview with Author.

35. Peter Gabel, Interview with Author. Also see Robert W. Gordon, "Some Critical Theories of Law and Their Critics," in *The Politics of Law: A Progressive Critique, Third Edition*, ed. David Kairys (New York: Basic Books, 1998): 654.

36. On other vocal Crits who advocated for this type of movement approach, see David Kairys, "Structure of CCLS," January 28, 1983; Kennedy, Interview; Jeremy Paul, "CLS 2001," *Cardozo Law Review*, Vol. 22, No. 3–4 (2001).

37. Unger (2015), 21–22, 24.

38. Ibid., 26.

39. Ibid., 29, 32.

40. Ibid., 29.

41. Ibid., 30.

42. Ibid., 32. In *Another Time, a Greater Task*, Unger crafts a partial theory of legal history, which we learn also mirrors the history of society and the evolution of our political structures. Unger argues that this history possesses "a characteristic rhythm: a recurrent success of three moments." The first moment of refoundation is characterized by a grand "institutional and ideological settlement," when new institutions are designed, ideologies enthroned, and "access to the resources, of economic capital, political power, and cultural authority" are negotiated and routinized. Unger connects this moment with certain periods in American history, such as our national founding, the Civil War and its aftermath, and the New Deal. The second moment—normalization—entrenches the institutional and ideological settlement, giving it greater definition and practical reinforcement. The final moment is what Unger terms "darkening." Darkening represents a sustained period of critical juncture, wherein the regnant political and legal arrangements become unbending, out of place, and hollow. This moment is inherently unstable and disorienting, as the

"authority and clarity" within our social order is jeopardized and vulnerable institutions begin to be challenged. Only a moment of refounding can remedy this chaos. Ibid., 17–21.

43. Within recent social scientific research, this type of collectivity has gone by an assortment of names, including network, scientific/intellectual movement (SIM), and school of thought. See Randall Collins, "On the Sociology of Intellectual Stagnation: The Late Twentieth Century in Perspective," *Theory, Culture & Society*, Vol. 9 (1992); Randall Collins, *The Sociology of Philosophies: A Global Theory of Intellectual Change* (Cambridge, MA & London: Belknap Press, 1998); Neil G. McLaughlin, "Why Do Schools of Thought Fail? Neo-Freudianism as a Case Study in the Sociology of Knowledge," *Journal of the History of the Behavioral Sciences*, Vol. 34, No. 2 (1998); Scott Frickel and Neil Gross, "A General Theory of Scientific/Intellectual Movements," *American Sociological Review*, Vol. 70, No. 22 (2005); Marion Blute and Paul Armstrong, "The Reinvention of Grand Theories of the Scientific/Scholarly Process," *Perspectives on Science*, Vol. 19, No. 4 (2011); Omar Lizardo, "Analytical Sociology's Superfluous Revolution," *Sociologica*, Vol. 1 (2012); Tom J. Waidzunas, "Intellectual Opportunity Structures and Science-Targeted Activism: Influence of the Ex-Gay Movement on the Science of Sexual Orientation," *Mobilization: An International Journal*, Vol. 18, No. 1 (2013); John N. Parker and Edward J. Hackett, "Hot Spots and Hot Moments in Scientific Collaborations and Social Movements," *American Sociological Review*, Vol. 77, No. 1 (2012); Johann Koehler, "Development and Fracture of a Discipline: Legacies of the School of Criminology at Berkeley," *Criminology*, Vol. 53, No. 4 (2015).

44. John Henry Schlegel, "Searching for Archimedes—Legal Education, Legal Scholarship, and Liberal Ideology," *Journal of Legal Education*, Vol. 34, No. 1 (1984) and Kennedy (2004).

45. Trubek, Interview.

46. Ibid.

47. Ibid. Also see Laura Kalman, *Yale Law School and the Sixties: Revolt and Reverberations* (Chapel Hill: University of North Carolina Press, 2005).

48. Kennedy, Interview; John H. Schlegel, Interview with Author; John Henry Schlegel, "Of Duncan, Peter, and Thomas Kuhn," *Cardozo Law Review*, Vol. 22, No. 3–4 (2001); Jay M. Feinman, "The Failure of Legal Education and the Promise of Critical Legal Studies," *Cardozo Law Review*, Vol. 6, No. 4 (1985).

49. Gordon, Interview. David Trubek echoes this point: "CLS was not part of a larger political effort in the United States... CLS was not connected to any politically oriented external network with its eyes on national politics." Trubek, Interview.

50. Kennedy, Interview; Peter Goodrich, "Duncan Kennedy as I Imagine Him: The Man, the Work, His Scholarship, and the Polity," *Cardozo Law Review*, Vol. 22, No. 3–4 (2001).
51. Minda (1989), 614.
52. Jamie Boyle, "Critical Legal Studies: A Young Person's Guide," March 1984: 13, 18.
53. See Ibid; Kennedy (2004), 204; David Kennedy, "Critical Theory, Structuralism and Contemporary Legal Scholarship," *New England Law Review*, Vol. 21, No. 2 (1986); Kennedy (2014), 587–89; David M. Trubek, "Foundational Events, Foundational Myths, and the Creation of Critical Race Theory, or How to Get Along with a Little Help from Your Friends," *Connecticut Law Review*, Vol. 43, No. 5 (2011): 1511; Schlegel (1984), 400; Paul (2001). On the strategy behind CLS recruitment, Duncan Kennedy says that Crits came to the conclusion that "we should put all of our energy into recruiting law professors and even the student recruitment should just be aimed at students who would become law professors... We were only interested in students because they might become law professors." Duncan Kennedy, Interview.
54. Robert W. Gordon, "Critical Legal Studies as a Teaching Method, Against the Background of the Intellectual Politics of Modern Legal Education in the United States," *Legal Education Review*, Vol. 1, No. 1 (1989): 75; Also see Robert W. Gordon, "Unfreezing Legal Reality: Critical Approaches to Law," *Florida State University Law Review*, Vol. 15, No. 2 (1987): 195–97.
55. Unger (2015), 5, 73.
56. Kennedy, Interview.
57. Jo L. Busser, Letter to Mark Tushnet, February 26, 1987.
58. Gary Minda, *Postmodern Legal Movements: Law and Jurisprudence at Century's End* (New York and London: New York University Press, 1995): 112; Also see Paul (2001); Brad Hudson, "Horwitz: A Critical Look at Studying Law," *Harvard Law Record*, Vol. 75, No. 8, November 19, 1982.
59. Gordon, Interview. Also see Arthur Austin, *The Empire Strikes Back: Outsiders and the Struggle over Legal Education* (New York and London: New York University Press, 1998): 84.
60. Rand E. Rosenblatt, Letter to Critical Legal Studies Organizing Committee, Summer Campers, and other interested People, September 8, 1982.
61. Gordon, Interview.
62. Karl E. Klare, Letter to Ed Sparer, January 4, 1982.
63. Ibid.
64. Conference on Critical Legal Studies, Newsletter, University of Wisconsin School of Law, n.d. Madison, WI.

CHAPTER 3

The Promise of CLS Retrenchment

Abstract This chapter reviews the concept of retrenchment and explains both how and why the CLS movement struggled to retrench the American legal academy. Central to the Crits' political efforts was the hope that current and future legal professionals would turn away from the legal liberal consciousness that dominated the American legal system.

Keywords Critical legal studies · Retrenchment · Law schools · Law professors · Legal consciousness · Legal liberalism

In the previous chapter, we uncovered both the origin of the CLS movement and also the type of collectivity that the Crits formed in the late 1970s. But was this rowdy band of legal leftists really all that important to the politics of the legal academy? Lest some worry that a trivial school of thought has been elevated too high (or low) by marking it as a legal movement, it might be helpful to keep in mind how the Crits have been recognized and remembered.

The CLS movement has been a strongly felt presence in the fights surrounding American legal development during the past few decades. While President of the United States, Ronald Reagan spoke publicly about the threat of CLS to the legal academy.[1] More recently, Ted Cruz

© The Author(s), under exclusive license to Springer Nature Switzerland AG 2021
P. Baumgardner, *Critical Legal Studies and the Campaign for American Law Schools,*
https://doi.org/10.1007/978-3-030-82378-8_3

reminded the Right of the powerful Crits who inhabited his law school alma mater. Speaking at an Americans for Prosperity rally in 2010, Cruz claimed that President Obama "would have made a perfect president of Harvard Law School" because "[t]here were fewer declared Republicans in the faculty when we were there than Communists! There was one Republican. But there were twelve who would say they were Marxists who believed in the Communists overthrowing the United States government."[2] This widely reported assertion mirrored a comment that the future US Senator and presidential candidate made in an earlier interview with a popular evangelical Christian magazine. When asked about his time at Harvard Law School, Cruz replied:

> Understanding Harvard Law School is very important to understanding our president, Barack Obama. He is very much a creature of Harvard Law. To understand what that means you have to understand that there were more self-declared communists on the Harvard faculty than there were Republicans. Every single idea this president has proposed in the nine months he's been in office has been orthodox wisdom in the Harvard faculty lounge... If you asked the Harvard faculty to vote on whether this nation should become a socialist nation, 80 percent of the faculty would vote yes and 10 percent would think that was too conservative.[3]

These remarks were widely reproduced amongst conservative news outlets, which worried that "Harvard, like so many institutions of higher learning across America, is infected with Marxist fellow travelers."[4] Conservative writer Matthew Vadum went so far as to track the different lawyers, legal scholars, and law schools "infected" by CLS.[5] Trumpeting one of the Right's greatest concerns about CLS, Vadum wrote:

> Imagine the chaos that would ensue if "Crits" dominated the judiciary. There would be no fixed rules. The only certain criterion for decisions would be so-called social justice, whatever that might mean on a particular day. As the judicial branch became an instrument of naked redistribution, Karl Marx would look up from his fiery torments and cheer as America degenerated into kleptocracy.[6]

Although this may appear to be little more than isolated, partisan fear-mongering confined to the fringes of the World Wide Web, we can turn to the US Supreme Court confirmation hearings of Elena Kagan in 2010 to unearth even more public consternation over CLS and its possible spread. Towards the beginning of Kagan's confirmation hearings, members of the Senate Judiciary Committee submitted written questions for the Supreme Court nominee to answer. Of these questions, the very first listed regarded the hiring of a Crit (Mark Tushnet) at Harvard Law School while Kagan was dean.[7] Senator Tom Coburn asked Kagan about Professor Tushnet's "approach to the law" and whether she would "endorse it" while a Supreme Court Justice.[8] Two questions later, Coburn was even more direct, explicitly interrogating Kagan about the CLS movement. He inquired: "Do you agree with the views of the Critical Legal Studies movement?" and "If not, with which of their views do you disagree?"[9] In the years since Kagan's confirmation hearings, additional questions related to CLS have found their way into judicial nomination hearings.[10]

In addition to the views of President Reagan, Senator Cruz, and Senator Coburn, numerous observers from the 1980s to the present have acknowledged CLS as a powerful leftist legal movement. In fact, it was CLS' explicit movement identity and Crits' collective actions that led many to view Crits as unsuitable for a place of professional learning. But before we tackle the fights over CLS that occurred in the legal academy, it would be wise to elucidate the central ideologies, political activities, and movement strategies of CLS during the 1980s.

This chapter will show that the Crits' core political actions reflected a primary movement goal of breaking the liberal consensus within the American legal system by retrenching the legal academy and destabilizing adjacent institutions. The CLS movement approached this goal by attacking law schools head-on and attempting to influence the professional legal consciousness that propped up the American legal system. Many Crits shared the belief that if the movement could, through the law schools, alter the legal consciousness of future "lawmakers and administrators, judges, legal scholars, practicing lawyers, and law teachers," serious political questioning and democratic deliberation would ensue, and meaningful change eventually would become possible across the American legal system.[11]

There was an assumption, of course, about the degree of influence that legal scholars—such as themselves—held over the legal profession and the future of the American legal system.[12] But the hope was that if the Crits could rip away the rose-tinted glasses, if new forms of critical legal scholarship, casebooks, and pedagogy could be wielded to demystify legal doctrines and dominant practices in the eyes of legal professionals, then a powerful wave of law school retrenchment could snowball into broader retrenchment across the legal system. Both legal professionals and the law would never be the same. Legal professionals would stand differently in relation to the Free Exercise Clause or to a federal district judge or to a law professor. And after this destabilization occurred—with legal consciousness unsettled and altered, and this or that legal practice shown in all its arbitrariness, contradictoriness, and political vulnerability—legal professionals very well may turn to more robust retrenchment projects and forms of revolutionary reconstruction.

In short, Crits' political actions were not so much about ideologizing institutions, such as the law schools, as they were about retrenching those institutions. The Crits' outsized reputation over the past forty years stems from the fact that the CLS movement brought retrenchment politics to the foreground of the legal academy. Through their teaching, scholarship, organizing, and everyday work within the law schools, the Crits challenged the dominant legal liberal characteristics of the American legal system and ended up standing as an existential threat to a heterogeneous mass of legal professionals and politicians in the United States during the 1980s.

REVIEWING RETRENCHMENT

A key reason why the CLS movement was perceived as threatening to people both inside and outside of the legal academy is because the Crits were waging a war of retrenchment throughout the 1980s. But what is retrenchment? And how might it apply to American law schools?

Since the mid-1990s, retrenchment has served as a popular concept for political scientists who are engaged in American political development (APD) research. With "features and dynamics that overlap with, but are also distinguishable from, the processes of political 'development'," retrenchment has proven to be a useful heuristic for meso-level analysis of American political institutions.[13] In addition to helping political scientists untangle the complex evolutionary patterns and internal reconstitutions of those institutions, the concept of retrenchment has advanced the core APD field objectives of mapping the nature and direction of institutional changes across time and space. As political scientists Karen Orren and Stephen Skowronek have outlined, within APD research "[p]attern identification is the sine qua non of the enterprise...Discovering patterns helps to locate the key components of a situation and demarcating them helps to identify meaningful points of change."[14] Political scientists who conduct APD research are fundamentally concerned with the direction of these historical patterns, in order to discover "whether the constant rearrangement of authority among and within institutions shows a movement over time in favor of some forms of principles over others. Direction is of interest in itself, objectively, because it speaks to the coherence of political change and to continuities presumed by the idea of historical construction."[15]

Recent APD research on retrenchment has explored the metamorphoses of various political institutions. For instance, Jacob Hacker and Eva C. Bertram have studied the retrenchment of federal welfare programs, focusing on the forms of conservative policy reform that occurred in the United States during the closing decades of the twentieth century.[16] Sarah Staszak has outlined the rule changes responsible for retrenching the federal judiciary and altering the procedures that govern access to the courts.[17] Robert G. Boatright has illustrated the role of state governments and political parties in shaping party primaries during the middle of the twentieth century.[18] Stephen B. Burbank and Sean Farhang have analyzed the diverse strategies deployed by the Right to retrench civil rights enforcement, with "counterrevolutionary" attempts being made through the executive, legislative, and judicial branches of the federal government beginning in the 1980s.[19]

But not all attempts at institutional change are attempts at retrenchment. Retrenchment represents a unique institutional process, "a distinctive and difficult political enterprise" that amounts to more than a temporary straying from entrenchment or an elemental component of state building.[20] Although the entrenchment, conservation, and decomposition of institutions may occur prior to retrenchment and open the door to retrenchment, retrenchment should not be "subsumed within a broader narrative of state development."[21] Instead, retrenchment is a sui generis process of intentional institutional erasure. This purposive process entails the intentional removal of the dominant ideas, personnel, and structural powers that undergird an institution.

The "three removals" of retrenchment—removals of dominant ideas, personnel, and structural powers—are what differentiate retrenchment from other consequential processes of institutional change. Removal of the dominant ideas of an institution requires the deletion of the fundamental ideas, values, rituals, and discourses that bolster an institution.

These dominant ideas establish the normative justifications for an institution, rationalize institutional conduct, and support the operations of an institution. Removing the dominant personnel within an institution amounts to an effective upending of the personal relations and resource arrangements within an institution. Common strategies associated with such removals include rejections of the official rules and procedures that undergird an institution, eliminations of prevailing systems of institutional organization, and—generally—restructurings of the chains of production that determine the desirable balances of costs, benefits, labor, provision of goods, and modes of accountability in an institution.

Removal of the dominant ideas and personnel of an institution overlaps with and pushes toward, a removal of the dominant structural powers that undergird an institution. Such a removal radically reorders an institution's structural capacities, loci of power, and means of governance. When the structural powers of a particular institution are intentionally erased through retrenchment, the grounding determinations of what that institution can do, what it will do, where it will do it, and how it will do it are broken down. The former locations, distributions, and exertions of power within an institution are unmade during retrenchment, resulting in new inward-looking and outward-looking manners of governance. Retrenchment provokes new ways through which an institution (and those institutional actors operating an institution) relates to itself and orders itself; this transformation also re-relates an institution to those outside of the institution.

Beyond these three removals, retrenchment requires no additional content. Institutional retrenchment can result in an institution of smaller size and scope, but retrenchment also can expand an institution.[22] Retrenchment can occur over the course of a single generation, but the erasure process also can stretch out across multiple generations. Retrenchment has been enacted through the labors of profoundly organized forces, linked together through clear and cohesive objectives, but there also are examples of this process occurring in a more diffuse, fractured, and roundabout fashion. Actors inside the halls of government can champion retrenchment, but those working outside of government can actively retrench institutions as well. Although some institutional retrenchments in American history have been highly visible and have gripped the public, Sarah Staszak's work reminds us of the "hidden" and "subterranean" aspects of many retrenchments, indicating that political scientists should look beyond the "'grand acts of politics'—landmark legislation or precedent-setting Supreme Court decisions—for evidence of retrenchment."[23]

Unpacking this sui generis process of intentional institutional erasure reveals that there are unexplored depths of retrenchment and rich possibilities for future APD research to track a different and more expansive political terrain impacted by retrenchers. Retrenchment helps to clarify both the nature and the direction of this form of institutional change—as a process that amounts to more than just moving backward, moving to the right, moving to repeal liberal advances, or moving to downsize the government. As a process of intentionally removing the dominant ideas, personnel, and structural powers that undergird an institution, retrenchment is not limited to conservative interruptions of an otherwise progressive American teleology.

Past political science scholarship on retrenchment also has gravitated to governmental institutions, with analysis oftentimes focusing on the direct impact of retrenchment on public policies. In fact, Jacob Hacker described his research into the "everyday forms of retrenchment" as an investigation into the "four modes of policy change."[24] Similarly, in *Ideas with Consequences: The Federalist Society and the Conservative Counterrevolution*, political scientist Amanda Hollis-Brusky conceived of the Federalist Society as a collection of political epistemic networks, which link "experts with policy-relevant knowledge who share certain beliefs and work to actively transmit and translate those beliefs into policy."[25] To analyze both the retrenchment successes and limitations of the Federalist Society, Hollis-Brusky assessed whether these policy experts and their policy prescriptions had infiltrated the US Supreme Court.

But although some examples of retrenchment do concern changes within the government, retrenchment is not restricted to governmental institutions. Throughout American history, politically significant retrenchment efforts also have taken place within nongovernmental institutions. In fact, the political efforts of the CLS movement supply a perfect case study of left-wing retrenchment conducted in nongovernmental institutions during the 1980s.

TRANSFORMING ANTI-LIBERALISM INTO RETRENCHMENT

With all of this talk of retrenchment, consciousness, and destabilization, it is easy for the Crit playbook to come across as overly conceptual.

But there are concrete and accessible reasons behind the Crits' political actions. To start, the mobilization of many Crits was rooted in a fundamental opposition. The Crits were unified in their critique of the American legal system's unholy relationship with legal liberalism. Legal liberalism was a capacious and omnipresent term in the CLS oeuvre, used both to describe and pinpoint a particular consensus consciousness of the legal system.[26]

The Crits were especially attuned to the consciousness of American legal professionals, and much of the CLS political project was formed around how Crits perceived current and future legal professionals' consciousness of the law. Crit law professor Karl Klare defined this CLS object of attention:

> By 'legal consciousness' I mean the vision of law and the world characteristic of the legal profession (or of a particular elite or other subgroup within it) at a given moment in history. 'Legal consciousness' imports not only explicit theorizing and discourse about law, but also conscious and unconscious assumptions and values pertaining to law and legal institutions…Legal consciousness includes the characteristic style or mode of reasoning of a group or epoch, the nature of the intellectual operations recognized as appropriate legal argument, the nature of the connection sought to be established between legal authority and legitimate adjudicatory outcomes, the manner in which legal problems are defined, and the types of evidence deemed relevant to legal inquiry. In sum, 'legal consciousness' refers to the constellations of assumptions underlying law and the structures and patterns of thought about law.[27]

Crits argued that a specific kind of liberal consensus existed within the American legal system. Legal liberalism represented the dominant legal consciousness within the United States or at least the leading lens through which legal professionals experienced the legal system. This professional class related to the legal system as if the system was characterized by reason, logic, symmetry, order, coherence, determinacy, and a general progressive mandate. Legal liberal consciousness revealed the American legal system as worthy of citizens' faith and respect, for the component elements of this system—especially the courts—protected individual rights, secured a just and orderly process of adjudicating disputes, and could be trusted to generate the reforms necessary for the promotion of social progress. As such, legal liberal consciousness led to the prioritization of court-based and individual rights-based attempts at producing social change. The creation and increase in individual rights represented the logical strategy for moving to a more egalitarian and democratic legal order.

According to the Crits, legal professionals also understood these liberal characteristics to be standards against which law was to be evaluated and maintained. If the Supreme Court deviated from the rational course, legal professionals would come to appreciate the Court's untoward development in light of their understanding of the judicial system as rational. Similarly, it would be lawyers' relational expectations of a logical and orderly training that would warn them of the perils associated with a disorderly and mismanaged legal education.

It was this liberal consciousness of our legal system that troubled many in the CLS movement, for Crits understood this consciousness to be the dominant legal consciousness among legal professionals and also a politically problematic consciousness.[28] For there had been grave injustice in the United States and caused by the United States in the 1960s and 1970s, which had been authorized and perpetuated by the country's legal system, during years of legal liberalism's dominance. How could it be that a positive orientation towards an ostensibly enlightened legal system, alongside a deep and abiding faith in judges, the just arc of the rule of law, and the rationality of legal processes could lead to—and vindicate—injustice? In the view of one Crit:

> My sense was that something that could be called liberal legalism was responsible for liberal professors, lawyers and judges acquiescing or collaborating in the war in Vietnam and the liberal failure to act aggressively against the oppression of blacks in urban spaces. But if legalism was responsible, the question was how. My intuition, very strongly felt, was that our mentor-teachers, the left-liberals, were trapped, in spite of their moderately good intentions. They were enveloped in a powerful consciousness of moderation, which they sincerely felt but which was also subtly self-interested. And which flatly contradicted how 'we' felt about things.[29]

Crits contended that legal professionals' consciousness of the American legal system was playing a significant role in the legitimation and reproduction of the system.[30] Legal liberal consciousness was a political rallying point for the Crits not only because this specific consciousness had led to legal professionals' undue faith in the orderliness, rationality, and naturalness of the American legal system, but also because it had a way of entrenching undesirable elements of the status quo into America's future legal system.[31] By falling under the "spell of the law," American legal professionals not only made the legal system appear organized and structured, but these professionals also gave the "loose, fluid, contingent, various miscellany of practices" within our legal system an air of inevitability and immunity to structural change.[32] This liberal consciousness was responsible for eviscerating attempts at massive legal reconstruction, by pushing legal professionals and the general population "into safe, 'liberal' channels incapable of achieving their transformative goals."[33] For even when a particular institution or legal practice appeared to grow inconsistent with the perceived virtues of the rest of the legal system, legal professionals would approach any changes from the legal liberal frame of respectable marginalism and mild technocratic reform.[34]

Notice that the Crits did not lack faith in the law, as numerous "critics of the Crits' have argued, declaring CLS a nihilistic movement hell-bent on pure destruction; the Crits thought that legal professionals" legal consciousness was awry and that the legal system in the United States was different than mainstream legal professionals made it appear to be and appear to have to be.[35] As one Crit noted during a speech on the movement, "We emphatically deny that there is any inevitable succession of structures...And we can freely replace them if we want to. 'Freely' not in the sense that it's easy, but in the sense that there's nothing inherent in the world that stands in the way if enough want to do it."[36]

The idea that a legal liberal consciousness would perpetuate the status quo by freezing the American legal system, leaving its institutions and practices sclerotic and entrenched, bothered the CLS movement more than any other political concern. As such, changing legal professionals' consciousness of the law became the principal project of the Crits. Changing consciousness represented, in its nucleus, professionals' fundamental re-relation to the legal system, away from a consciousness that "provides false legitimation when it conceals the violent, coercive, arbitrary and ugly faces of existing institutions" and "reinforces false necessity by suppressing the alternative arrangements, the more democratic, egalitarian, cooperative, liberating alternatives, that our legal norms and practices also make available."[37] But how could this re-relation be accomplished?

The Crits sought to change legal professionals' consciousness of the law predominantly through the retrenchment of the institution most

responsible for the production of legal professionals and the early education of those professionals: the law school. One Crit wrote, "The most
immediate setting of our transformative activity is also on its face the
most modest: the law schools."[38] This particular institution was an essential target of retrenchment, two Crits wrote, because "[l]egal education
is dominated by consciousness or ideology about law, lawyering, and
learning that permeates every aspect of the law school. Curriculum and
classroom style, personal relations, and student assessment reflect a particular view of the world. That view is put forth as rational, professional, and
just."[39]

Because the dominant legal liberal consciousness within the legal
academy presented the legal system as rational, professional, and just,
some of the Crits' academic colleagues saw the system as "untrans-
formable" and personally retreated to "an inward distance from a reality
whose yoke, according to them, cannot be broken."[40] But the Crits
resisted this scholarly detachment. Indoctrinating law students with such
professional aloofness had the deleterious effect of making highly contingent legal doctrines and political arrangements appear necessary. Instead,
Crits asserted that "law is politics, all the way down," and the unjust
hierarchies and power inequalities present within the United States could
be remedied by "constructing a new consciousness of law" and having
law students and young lawyers come to understand the law for the
pliable and contestatory terrain that it is.[41] The Crits understood that
the legal academy was not shackled to its production and reproduction of legal liberal consciousness. The law schools' process of educating
law students and preparing lawyers was a political process—embedded
with political goals and serving particular political outcomes—and also
a mutable process. So if legal liberal consciousness needed to go, the
academy needed to be retrenched.

To CLS, the revolution to break the liberal consensus within the
American legal system would run through the law school. Not only was
retrenchment of the legal academy key to shifting the consciousness of
current and future legal professionals, but law schools also provided the
perfect home base for connecting to the bar, organizing and mobilizing
professors and students in the movement, developing intellectual capital,
and piloting new political activities. As one Crit professor explained to
Clark Byse, a professor at Harvard Law School, "CLS types" changing
the American legal system had to include more than just "tinkering with
this or that rule or field."[42] Real change required "suggesting deeper

change," with new visions of how different building blocks within the legal system would operate, such as "a shift from one vision of the city or the labor union (worker management, etc.) to another vision, from one vision of the role of courts to another vision."[43]

RETRENCHING THE LEGAL ACADEMY

Removing the dominant ideas, personnel, and structural powers that undergirded the legal academy would require a wholesale deconstruction of the liberal shibboleths propping up the nation's law schools, as well as a complete erasure of the orthodox manner in which the legal professionals working within the law schools related to the law schools and to the broader legal system. But what, exactly, would this entail?

Due to the organizational flexibility of CLS, it can be difficult to explain the Crits' retrenchment project. The movement was highly decentralized, identifiable by its "constant attention to the art of organizing" and also its "refusal to set analytic or programmatic group priorities among types and styles of transformative activism."[44] As one Crit explained, the movement prioritized localized struggles, instead of a set of centrally coordinated and nationally imposed reforms: "Radical reformation of this vast miscellany of contingent practices isn't likely to come about through drawing blueprints to replace one fictitiously described abstract order with another...but by pressing against thousands of local situations of constraint for the fuller realization of the liberating possibilities that are already immanent in this jungle of orders."[45]

With only a minimal degree of top-down activity orchestration, the CLS movement instead relied on friendships, school networks, and local support among likeminded legal scholars and law students to coordinate different political actions and push the legal movement forward.[46] Despite this organizational looseness, the movement remained united:

> [W]e are united in that we would like our work, in so far as it is possible, to help in modest ways to realize the potential we believe exists to transform the practices of the legal system to help make this a more decent, equal, solidary society—less intensively ordered by hierarchies of class, status, "merit," race, and gender—more decentralized, democratic, and participatory.[47]

Throughout the 1980s, the Crits engaged in a variety of political activities directed at the retrenchment of the legal academy and, in the process, the reorientation and radicalization of the next generation of American legal professionals.

As a movement comprised largely of professional academics, many Crits directed their legal scholarship to the task of removing the dominant ideas percolating within American law schools and poking holes in the intellectual justification for the current institutional formation of the legal academy. If both the production of legal knowledge and legal knowledge itself could never be neutral, then it was essential to the Crits that they fight for their preferred forms of knowledge and knowledge production. Critical legal scholarship during the 1980s was impressive, in terms of both sheer volume and ability to grab attention. Writing in 1989 about the movement, law professor Allan C. Hutchinson admitted that "its presence is strong and incontestable: around 700 articles and books in print can be grouped loosely under the rubric of CLS."[48] As another law professor from the period recalls, Crits' scholarship "was aggressive advocacy—practically every sentence was a political statement, and even bland footnotes had been politicized."[49]

Many of the most skillful works of critical legal scholarship included robust historical analysis, which bolstered the Crits' political advocacy. Critical legal historiography took great pains to unearth law's specificity within particularized contexts. The Crits asked how law operated and held power within specific social, political, and historical spaces. How, within those spaces, did critiques of law affect law's operation?[50] And, in the contemporary American context, if the nation's legal system did not merely reflect American society, but also played an essential role in constituting that society, then "[l]egal practices and discourses can be understood as a terrain of conflict between social visions, as a 'medium' or 'field' in which to pursue moral and political projects and to articulate radical visions of democracy and equality."[51] As such, critical legal scholarship could play a leading role in the United States "to articulate and defend alternative, 'counterhegemonic' social visions within legal discourses and thereby to inspire/mobilize opposition and resistance."[52]

Deviationist doctrine and trashing were two common forms of CLS scholarship during the 1980s, forms which many Crits wielded to subvert the fundamental values, rituals, and discourses within the legal academy. Deviationist doctrine was meant to show "the distinctive coexistence of dominant and deviant solutions in each branch of law," reveal the relent-less doctrinal competitions that were always struggling to reorganize and reorder the legal system, and emphasize the different doctrinal possibili-ties that existed under the surface of each field of American law.[53] Crits, such as Roberto Unger and Duncan Kennedy, believed that these hidden alternatives could be used to openly contest and "reinvent doctrine" in a manner that would make entire legal fields "more democratic, more egalitarian, and more communal."[54]

For example, in the fields of civil rights law and labor law, Crits such as Gary Peller, Alan Freeman, and Karl Klare argued that moving away from the dominant legal liberal consciousness could open up avenues of thinking that would not de-radicalize everyday workers, but instead would highlight deviant legal doctrines and develop new prac-tices that enhanced the democratic power of workers. The possibility of legally protecting expressions of workplace democracy and worker self-determination would require strong safeguards for racial and ethnic minorities. And the broadened civil rights safeguards for these Ameri-cans would not be piecemeal, individuated, or justified on the basis of cost-effectiveness. Crits argued passionately in their scholarship that the broadening of labor rights and civil rights must do more than secure new indeterminate and individual rights, if a group plans on toppling illegitimate hierarchies and inequalities in society.[55]

Crits cautioned against new, contentless rights being deployed as a liberal panacea by the state, because Crits were sensitive to the ways in which legal liberalism could engender group pacification and permit new forms of legal subjugation in the workplace. In a letter to Victor Rabinowitz, Duncan Kennedy explained:

> Liberal legalism, the struggle to secure people's "rights", as though rights were the be-all and end-all, at once the solution to the problem of injustice and the imaginary entities that could tell us what strategy to pursue, all that seems to me useful tactically, but also as having serious drawbacks. If people believe that the issue is "rights" rather than the refashioning of relationships, the redistribution of power, and the utopian invention of new forms or work and love, then I think the liberal rights reform strategy is a kind of diversion or a dead end.[56]

By wielding deviationist doctrine, Crits sought to revive doctrinal alter-natives, develop new legal claims, and pressure legal professionals to rethink the dominant precedents and historical trajectories in American law. Dozens of sessions at CLS national meetings were dedicated to unearthing the dormant principles and doctrinal solutions that could be brought to the surface in diverse areas of America law, from health law to administrative law, constitutional law to labor law.[57]

Trashing was another common scholarly practice among the Crits. More playful, avant-garde, and sardonic than deviationist doctrine, CLS regularly "trashed" fellow law professors, their scholarship, and their political role in rationalizing and reproducing the hierarchies and unequal power relations that existed in the American legal system. CLS trashers poked, prodded, and attacked fellow "intellectuals," riling up mainstream law professors and their vulnerable "prestige."[58] Trashing took many forms: published and unpublished comedies, dialogues, cartoons, "silli-nesses," psychological assessments, and even a mock movie review that highlighted Ronald Dworkin's new high-budget, action-packed block-buster book.[59] To those law professors who opposed trashing, believing that academic scholarship should be dignified and serious, two trashers responded:

> So is trashing. It makes crystal clear that the can upended is not a treasure chest, but a cardboard box full of the same old rags and empty bottles... What we trash are the same old liberal self-delusions that have been slung around here for years. We trash to make it apparent that reprocessed apolo-getics for liberal legalism of the kind you have sold for years simply won't wash anymore. It is time to be serious about race and sex and class: about power. What we trash is simply not serious and we refuse to act as if it were![60]

But although the Crits were prolific scholars who understood their writ-ings to be important vehicles for transforming the legal academy, the CLS movement was not intent on being a school of thought, and the collectivity amounted to much more than scholars penning scholarship. Although "the group was collectively working toward a new definition of the intellectual map," the movement offered more than navel-gazing or intra-academic squabbling.[61] As the program for the Third Annual Conference on Critical Legal Studies declared, CLS represented both a scholarly and an activist community. It was dedicated to "the development of a theory of radical law practice."[62] Multiple members of the movement powerfully voiced this commitment to extending their academic work beyond the pages of the law review.[63] They were sensitive to those who thought that "CLS work" was "'academic' rather than 'practical'" and they criticized leftists who "think they can get more out of study than it's possible to get. They've gone to the library, and they're determined that by the time they get back from the library, they're going to have settled the problem."[64]

The Crits were quick to point out that the movement was not a group of scholars who routinely met up to formulate and refine some grand theory of the law. Instead, the movement aspired to mount a campaign of anti-legal liberalism local politics, which would build counterhegemonic forces strong enough to retrench the legal academy and alter the future of the American legal system. Crits planned to do radical politics where they were, with the hopes of transforming their workplaces. Crits brought political conflicts to the fore within the academy, instead of repressing them in the name of good manners.

Teaching was one of the primary ways in which the Crits engaged in left oppositionist activities, which organized and mobilized both leftist scholars and students. Crits' teaching was understood to be a principal mechanism for erasing the dominant personal relations and resource arrangements within the law schools. Unlike their "anti-intellectual" colleagues, who demonstrated "an unwillingness to reflect on the goals of legal education, the content of the curriculum, the methods of teaching, and the ability of law school graduates to practice law competently," the Crits were acutely aware of the political assumptions and practical possibilities associated with educating law students.[65]

Law school teaching presented an opportunity to approach and educate large groups of young Americans who were seeking to become political elites and hold immense power in society. The Crits were aware of the kingmaking potential of their elite institutions and the revolving door effects that they could generate from their professional perches. Accordingly, constructing a critical legal pedagogy was one of the central objectives of the CLS movement during the 1980s. At one CLS summer camp meeting, a small handout titled "The American Critical Legal Studies Movement In A Nutshell" was distributed.[66] A hybrid underground history-cum-political program for the movement, this foldable and pocket-sized handout listed Crit professors' "struggle for legitimacy in mainstream courses" and "taking common law doctrinal fields seriously as locus of conflict" as two of the "[p]rototypical cls activities."[67]

Crits held discussion groups at CCLS meetings to help each other work through critical teaching methods and materials for the contracts, constitutional law, criminal law, and torts 1L courses.[68] For instance, at the Fourth National Conference on Critical Legal Studies at the University at Buffalo School of Law, breakout groups spent hours sharing and discussing Crits' "course outlines, syllabi, letters describing the participants' interests and concerns."[69] Several years later, teaching materials and extensive reports on legal education were provided and discussed at the Seventh National Conference on Critical Legal Studies, which was dedicated to the theme "From Criticism to Reconstruction."[70] These materials covered multiple topics, including methods for teaching contracts, advice for teaching constitutional law, professional responsibilities of leftist law professors, revisions to the corporate law curriculum, and information related to deviationist doctrine. The movement's newsletters also assisted in this cardinal educational project, by giving information about different Crits' course syllabi and even publishing articles on CLS "Teaching Techniques."[71]

The pedagogical designs of Crit retrenchers reflected the movement's attempts to reshape the core curriculum of the law school, teach students the distributional consequences and power relations codified in American law, and explore how to revise those codifications. A large part of removing the dominant personal relations within the law schools relied on "getting students early"—engaging and radicalizing law students through the foundational law school courses (e.g., torts, contracts, property, criminal law), courses about areas of the law that first-year law students may have thought were rational, orderly, settled, and already aimed towards the good of society. Crits worked to subvert the consensus liberal "message" and "reasoning" taught in law school classrooms, which reassured law students that "if you are fair, reasonably competent, neutral, and unbiased, the process will produce a legally required, socially optimal, correct result."[72] As one Crit described in a letter from 1979, "What we want to do is...try to create or reinforce a sense of unease in our students. Especially with first-year students, and the limited time I have them in class, I try to shatter the myths they bring with them to law school and prevent them from adopting any of the traditional myths of legal liberalism."[73]

Crits such as Robert Gordon enjoined professors and students alike to engage in a creative practice of "Challenge and Experimentation": The class should survey the status quo in a particular area of law, dissect the existing doctrine, recognize the "multiple alternative interpretations" and sites of contingency and ongoing struggle in its "teeming jungle of multiple, overlapping, contradictory systems," and then work together to unearth the possibilities for "a more democratic, egalitarian and solidary vision of social life" if the right pieces, legal claims, and actions were pressed in that legal field *today*.[74] Where elements of the legal system were sanctioning oppression and injustice in American society, Crits sought to show students that the law also could be used against the law—that lawyers could rely on the law as a vehicle for social transformation.

Whereas past generations of students had been taught that "thinking like a lawyer" demanded blind identification with the judge or with the client on any given legal matter, the Crits were willing to reveal the judge to be little more than the Wizard of Oz, while also stressing that "client service" should be more ethically complex than many law professors let on in the classroom.[75] Crits believed that lawyers should do more—and be more—in order to promote a just legal order. By highlighting the extraordinary degree of doctrinal uncertainty and non-neutrality for students, the Crits' pedagogical approaches emphasized the omnipresence of choice within the legal system and within future legal development.[76] Similarly, Karl Klare wrote about the political objectives behind his own critical teaching:

> In capsule form, the goals of critical legal pedagogy are—to disrupt the socialization process that occurs during legal education; to unfreeze entrenched habits of mind and deconstruct the false claims of necessity which constitute so-called 'legal reasoning'; to urge students to see their life's work ahead as an opportunity to unearth and challenge law's dominant ideas about society, justice, and human possibility and to infuse legal rules and practices with emancipatory and egalitarian content.[77]

If the dominant legal consciousness in the United States retained its power through the forms of socialization, self-presentation, language, and legal reasoning practiced and taught in the law schools, then the Crits would have to resist those orthodox behaviors and seemingly mundane practices.[78] Crits believed that their teaching could profoundly influence their students' consciousness of the law and have a considerable impact on these future lawyers' understandings of the American legal system, daily work within the legal profession, and what "ethical and political solutions" and goals were legally possible. This semi-indoctrinatory strategy played a leading role in the Crits' attempts to retrench the law schools.[79]

Their critical legal pedagogy sought to reconfigure the costs and benefits of a legal education, while changing the nature of the goods that law schools provided to their client students.

Finally, it is crucial to keep in mind that the Crits' pedagogy was about more than cognitive development and the mastery of legal rules; it also was about praxis. Crits showed students that alternative legal systems were possible, and they demonstrated the materials that could be deployed for retrenching current systems and building anew. Crit professors themselves sought to serve as models, by offering new legal visions to their students and to fellow scholars. If successful, these heterodox approaches to legal training would go a long way in rearticulating the standard relationship between law faculty and students and advancing leftist movement lawyering. "For the most part, students did not enroll in our classes because of their or our politics. Instead, they developed an interest in radical politics—if at all during law school—often as a result of our classes," one Crit recollects.[80] As we will see in the next chapter, this approach worked in some of the nation's leading law schools during the early 1980s.

Beyond scholarship and teaching, Crits engaged in various forms of workplace politics that sought to radically reorder the legal academy's structural capacities, loci of power, and means of governance. Across multiple law schools, Crits tried to achieve a degree of "left workplace self-determination" by building a community of retrenchers, developing recruitment efforts and mentorships, reconstituting law school personnel, fighting to reform courses and academic requirements, and participating in countless talks, debates, symposia, and miscellaneous forms of professional activism and public provocations.[81]

To build up a community of retrenchers, the Crits established dozens of conferences, camps, and reading groups throughout the 1980s. CLS conferences brought together hundreds of Crits and bred solidarity, as current and potential members engaged in conversation, made presentations, debated, received teaching and political instruction, and conducted movement planning. Once conferences concluded, many members went back home and began smaller reading groups with fellow Crits and interested law students, law professors, and lawyers.[82] In a letter to Karl Klare, Lucie White discussed the importance of "working out a common perspective, common questions, a common vocabulary" in CLS.[83] In the letter, White detailed how "ongoing discussion, study groups between these large meetings are <u>essential</u> to the project we're talking about undertaking."[84] The Crits also held more than ten "summer camps" and "winter camps," where members would read each other's work and ground themselves in foundational texts of the New Left. As one Crit recalled:

> By far the best way to get to know the Crits was to go to a CLS Summer Camp. CLS Summer camp was open to anyone interested in CLS. At Summer camp one could live and party with the Crits for three or four days and nights (hardly anyone ever really slept since no one wanted to miss out on the late night fun). There were lots of interesting discussions about law, politics, legal educations, etc., lots of horsing around, lots of opportunities to meet really cool folks, and always the possibility of having a sudden, intuitive moment of connectedness—what "Crits" called 'intersubjective Zap.'... When compared to the American Association of Law Schools annual profession meetings for law professors, or Law and Economics, or whatever, CLS Summer Camp was more like going to Woodstock than a law conference. It was also one of those life-changing experiences that forever altered one's perspective about law and legal education.[85]

Throughout the 1980s, Crits also penned *Newsletters of the Conference on Critical Legal Studies*. Filled with personal letters, news on campus fights, activism suggestions, organizational criticisms, teaching materials, conference alerts, and lists of recent CLS scholarship, these newsletters functioned as the official bulletin of the movement. All of the aforementioned movement events and tools fostered close friendships and ideological alliances, and they sustained CLS for years of political action.

A related form of workplace politics was the development of recruitment efforts and mentorship opportunities for younger scholars. As one Crit boldly claimed when speaking at a CLS conference: "Perhaps the best test is whether our political message is sufficiently organized and general to teach students arguments to use in other classes against our colleagues."[86] To influence the next wave of legal professionals, Crits identified fellow travelers, offered close advising to promising students, invited guests to CLS meetings and conferences, began local reading groups, helped place young leftists in academic posts, and supported students' political activities through "everything from being the official faculty advisor to left groups to consulting about radical initiatives in which some faculty knowledge of the likely reaction of the school or university administration might be helpful (building occupations and sit-ins, for example)."[87] In an interview, Duncan Kennedy addressed this transgenerational dynamic within CLS:

> It was part of our politics to form politically based bonds with students who were criticizing the school in general and our collegial opponents in particular. That violated the very basic professional norm that your first loyalty was to the institution and to your colleagues however much you disagreed with them. That wasn't my view. I was more loyal to the left counter-hegemonic project than to Harvard Law School and its faculty.[88]

These recruitment efforts and mentorships spurred CLS growth and helped the movement during its decade-long retrenchment fight across the American legal academy. In fact, the workplace practices that have become most closely associated with CLS—and which most clearly demonstrate the movement's effort to unmake the regnant distributions of power within the legal academy—pertain to Crits' attempts to recon-stitute law school personnel. Across multiple law schools, Crits engaged in vocal, long-term fights to "reintegrate the communities we live in along explicitly egalitarian lines rather than along the rationalized hier-archical lines that currently integrate them."[89] In so doing, the Crits were modeling within the academy their broader vision for the Amer-ican legal system, to "[s]upport redistribution of power between social groups in every conceivable institutional setting by the method of seeking to alter the legal rules that structure interaction, bargaining, and power relations."[90]

Crits fought hard to increase the number of female and minority faculty members, while also adding leftist scholars to law school payrolls. In order to establish the legal academy as a "counterhegemonic enclave" for the racially, sexually, and ideologically underrepresented, Crits gained enough strength at several law schools to influence the faculty appointment process for years.[91] Crits also sought to implement curricular reforms and recast academic requirements within the law schools. Noteworthy goals included the elimination of the Socratic method; faculty control over law school admissions, with the hope that student selection would become a powerful weapon in weakening unjust professional hierarchies and achieving social equality; the implementation of no-hassle passes and grading policies meant to ease student strain and constrain traditionalist professors who lorded over arbitrary and unfair classrooms; and fundamentally reworking the curricular tracks, course materials, and teaching strategies within the law schools. Instead of legal education amounting to years of "learning the law"—memorizing the ostensibly static structure, internal rationality, and logical coherence of each legal field—Crits wanted to communicate the indeterminacy and openness of legal fields, introduce room for professional creativity, and highlight the valuable role that lawyers play in crafting the law. This more progressive pedagogical mission corresponded with CLS suggestions for law school tracks that prioritized clinical education, legal theory, and forms of learning linked to real-world politics and social activism.[92]

Although, by the mid-1980s, the sheer size of the CLS movement aided the fight for these retrenchment goals, several Crits also attempted to gain administrative power within their respective law schools. Paul Brest—a law professor who presented at several CLS meetings and attended CLS summer camps—became dean of Stanford Law School. The secretary of CLS, Mark Tushnet, applied to become dean of Georgetown University Law Center. In an outline for his deanship application, Tushnet explicitly stated that one of the main reasons that he was applying concerned CLS. Tushnet believed that his deanship would be a significant contribution to the CLS movement, noting that it would exemplify the movement's role as a "positive force in legal education."[93]

Finally, in order to shift the consciousness of current and future legal professionals, the Crits also needed to re-relate the academy to those outside of the academy. Accordingly, many Crits took the movement struggle beyond the walls of the law schools. The external activism of CLS included a wide range of public mobilizations, "to operate in the interspace of artifacts, gestures, speeches and rhetoric, histrionics, drama, all very paradoxical, soap opera, pop culture, all that kind of stuff."[94] Crits engaged in interviews with the popular media, gave talks outside of the law school, suggested new forms of leftist legal practice for lawyers, made subversive artwork, leafleted, and supported community organizers.[95] As we will see in the following chapters, these multifarious retrenchment actions brought tremendous attention to the CLS movement during the 1980s. This attention generated a boom in movement forces and a rise in CLS influence, but it also led many legal professionals across the United States to fear the Crits' direct challenge to legal academy.

"Where the Real Political Action Is"

Throughout the 1980s, the CLS movement sought to retrench the American legal academy by removing the dominant ideas, personnel, and structural powers that undergirded the academy. In doing so, the Crits intentionally prioritized attacks on nongovernmental institutions—the law schools—over direct assaults on governmental institutions. This political project must have puzzled some, but the Crits believed that their attacks were essential to dismantling the institutions most responsible for the production of legal professionals and the early education of those professionals. Through its efforts to retrench the legal academy, the CLS movement hoped to veer legal professionals' consciousness away from the consensus legal liberal consciousness of the era. As Mark Tushnet put it:

> [T]he academy has had difficulty understanding how people could be interested in the law without being interested in influencing policymakers. Yet, in light of the substantive political views associated with cls, that seems to be the case for cls... People associated with cls have a different sense of where the real political action is, and have started to develop forms of legal theorizing and legal practice that orient themselves toward mobilizing communities for more than incremental change.[96]

Notes

1. Ronald Reagan, "Remarks to the Federalist Society for Law and Public Policy Studies, September 9, 1988." *Ronald Reagan Presidential Library*. https://www.reaganlibrary.gov/research/speeches/090988h.
2. Jane Mayer, "Is Senator Ted Cruz Our New McCarthy?" *The New Yorker*, February 22, 2013. http://www.newyorker.com/news/daily-comment/is-senator-ted-cruz-our-new-mccarthy.
3. Marvin Olasky, "All Together Now," *The World*, October 23, 2009. https://world.wng.org/2009/10/all_together_now.
4. Matthew Vadum, "We Have Ted Cruz's List: Harvard Law Really *Is* Littered with Communists." *American Thinker*, March 5, 2013. http://www.americanthinker.com/articles/2013/03/we_have_ted_cruzs_list_harvard_law_really_islittered_with_communists.html.
5. Ibid.; Matthew Vadum, "Ted Cruz May Not Have a List of Communists at Harvard Law, But I Do," *PJ Media*, March 8, 2013. https://pjmedia.com/blog/ted-cruz-may-not-have-a-list-of-communists-at-harvard-law-but-i-do/.
6. Vadum (2013).

7. "Written Questions of Senator Tom Coburn, M.D.," U.S. Senate Committee on the Judiciary, July 2, 2010. http://www.scotusblog.com/wp-content/uploads/2010/07/Written.pdf.

8. Ibid.

9. Ibid.

10. See, e.g., *Confirmation Hearings on Federal Appointments*, Senate Hearing 113-515, Committee on the Judiciary, United States Senate, November 20, 2013. https://www.govinfo.gov/content/pkg/CHRG-113shrg24007/html/CHRG-113shrg24007.htm.

11. See, e.g., Gordon (1998), 650; Alan Hunt, "The Theory of Critical Legal Studies," *Oxford Journal of Legal Studies*, Vol. 6, No. 1 (1986).

12. Richard W. Bauman, *Ideology and Community in the First Wave of Critical Legal Studies* (Toronto: University of Toronto Press, 2002): 55–56.

13. Sarah Staszak, "Institutions, Rulemaking, and the Politics of Judicial Retrenchment," *Studies in American Political Development*, Vol. 24, No. 2 (2010): 170.

14. Karen Orren and Stephen Skowronek, *The Search for American Political Development* (Cambridge, UK and New York: Cambridge University Press, 2004): 7.

15. Ibid., 172–73.

16. Jacob S. Hacker, "Privatizing Risk without Privatizing the Welfare State: The Hidden Politics of Social Policy Retrenchment in the United States," *American Political Science Review*, Vol. 98, No. 2 (2004); Eva C. Bertram, "The Institutional Origins of 'Workfarist' Social Policy," *Studies in American Political Development*, Vol. 21, No. 2 (2007).

17. Sarah Staszak, *No Day in Court: Access to Justice and the Politics of Judicial Retrenchment* (New York and Oxford: Oxford University Press, 2015).

18. Robert G. Boatright, "Retrenchment or Reform? Changes in Primary Election Laws, 1928–70," *Polity*, Vol. 51, No. 1 (2019).

19. Stephen B. Burbank and Sean Farhang, *Rights and Retrenchment: The Counterrevolution Against Federal Litigation* (New York: Cambridge University Press, 2017); Stephen B. Burbank and Sean Farhang, "Retrenching Civil Rights Litigation: Why the Court Succeeded Where Congress Failed," in *The Rights Revolution Revisited: Institutional Perspectives on the Private Enforcement of Civil Rights in the U.S.*, ed. Lynda G. Dodd (Cambridge and New York: Cambridge University Press, 2018).

20. Paul Pierson, *Dismantling the Welfare State? Reagan, Thatcher, and the Politics of Retrenchment* (Cambridge, UK: Cambridge University Press, 1994): 1.

21. Staszak (2015), 27–28.

22. See Bertram (2007).

23. Staszak (2015), 7–8.

24. Hacker (2004), 246, 248, 257.
25. Hollis-Brusky (2015), 10–11, 22–23.
26. For representative CLS views on legal liberalism, see Kelman (1987); Duncan Kennedy, "First Year Law Teaching as Political Action," *Law & Social Problems*, Vol. 1 (1980); Lee Christie, "Prof. Frug Urges Critical Look at Law," *Harvard Law Record*, December 3, 1982: 9; Minda (1995).
27. Karl Klare, "Contracts Jurisprudence and the First-Year Casebook," *New York University Law Review*, Vol. 54, No. 4 (1979): 876–77. Also see Bauman (2002), 49–50; David M. Trubek, "Where the Action Is: Critical Legal Studies and Empiricism," *Stanford Law Review*, Vol. 36, No. 1–2 (1984); Duncan Kennedy, "Toward an Historical Understanding of Legal Consciousness: The Case of Classical Legal Thought in America, 1850–1940," in *Research in Law and Sociology, Volume 3*, ed. Stephen Spitzer (Greenwich, CT: JAI Press, 1980); Duncan Kennedy, *The Rise and Fall of Classical Legal Thought* (Washington, DC: Beard Books, 2006); Alan David Freeman, "Legitimizing Racial Discrimination Through Antidiscrimination Law: A Critical Review of Supreme Court Doctrine," *Minnesota Law Review*, Vol. 62, No. 6 (1978); Peter Gabel, "Intention and Structure in Contractual Conditions: Outline of a Method for Critical Legal Theory," *Minnesota Law Review*, Vol. 61, No. 4 (1977); Duncan Kennedy, "The Structure of Blackstone's Commentaries," *Buffalo Law Review*, Vol. 28, No. 2 (1979); Peter Gabel, "Book Review: Taking Rights Seriously," *Harvard Law Review*, Vol. 91, No. 1 (1977).
28. See Gabel and Harris (1983); Minda (1995), 110, 115; Gary Peller, "The Metaphysics of American Law," *California Law Review*, Vol. 73, No. 4 (1985); Karl E. Klare, "Judicial Deradicalization of the Wagner Act and the Origins of Modern Legal Consciousness, 1937–1941," *Minnesota Law Review*, Vol. 62, No. 3 (1978); Gary Minda, "Neil Gotanda and the Critical Legal Studies Movement," *Asian Law Journal*, Vol. 4 (1997).
29. Tor Krever, Carl Lisberger and Max Utzschneider, "Law on the Left: A Conversation with Duncan Kennedy," *Unbound: Harvard Journal of the Legal Left*, Vol. 10 (2015): 9.
30. William N. Eskridge, Jr., and Gary Peller, "The New Public Law Movement: Moderation as a Postmodern Cultural Form," *Michigan Law Review*, Vol. 89, No. 4 (1991): 781–82; Mark Tushnet, "Critical Legal Studies: A Political History," *Yale Law Journal*, Vol. 100, No. 5 (1991): 1527; Gordon (1998), 649.
31. Peller (1985); John Henry Schlegel, "CLS Wasn't Killed by a Question," *Alabama Law Review*, Vol. 58, No. 5 (2007): 973–74. Faith in the justice and orderliness of law was a calling card of the legal process tradition. See, e.g., White (1984), 661–62; Unger (1986); Minda (1995); Kelman (1987); David Kairys, "Introduction," in *The Politics of Law: A Progressive*

Critique, Third Edition, ed. David Kairys (New York: Basic Books, 1998): 1–3; Also see Peter Gabel, "Reification in Legal Reasoning," in *Research in Law and Sociology, Volume 3*, ed. Stephen Spitzer (Greenwich, CT: JAI Press, 1980); Gordon (1998); William N. Eskridge, Jr. and Philip P. Frickey, "The Making of 'The Legal Process'," *Harvard Law Review*, Vol. 107, No. 8 (1994).

32. Teles (2008), 24; Gabel (1977), 605; Gordon (1998), 650 and Kairys (1998), 12.
33. Teles (2008), 192.
34. Tushnet (1991), 1528, 1533 and Gordon (1998), 647–48.
35. According to David Kairys: "We do not, as some progressive approaches have in the past, dismiss the law as a sham or a subterfuge; our criticism takes seriously the law's doctrines, principles, methods, and promises. Critical analysis exposes the law's proclamations of inevitability, reason, and logic as false necessity and false legitimacy, and opens up the possibility of alternatives. This provides both a deeper understanding of law and society and an essential tool for engaging in the immediate, ongoing contest over values and priorities within the law." Kairys (1998), 16. Also see, Robert H. Bork, *The Tempting of America: The Political Seduction of the Law* (New York: Touchstone, 1990); Paul D. Carrington, "Of Law and the River," *Journal of Legal Education*, Vol. 34, No. 2 (1984); Frug, "McCarthyism and Critical Legal Studies," *Harvard Civil Rights-Civil Liberties Law Review*, Vol. 22, No. 2 (1987); Unger (2015).
36. Mark Tushnet, Talk on the CLS Movement, Unpublished notes, n.d. 5. On file with Author.
37. Gordon (1998), 652.
38. Unger (1986), 112.
39. Feinman and Marc Feldman, "Pedagogy and Politics," *Georgetown Law Journal*, Vol. 73 (1985): 926. Also see Marc Feldman and Jay M. Feinman, "Legal Education: Its Cause and Cure," *Michigan Law Review*, Vol. 82, No. 4 (1984): 923–27.
40. Unger (1986), 113.
41. Tushnet (1991), 1526 and Feinman and Feldman (1985), 877.
42. Clark Byse, "Fifty Years of Legal Education," *Iowa Law Review*, Vol. 71 (1986): 1084.
43. Ibid.
44. Duncan Kennedy, "The American Critical Legal Studies Movement in a Nutshell," June 1984: 4. Also see Krever, Lisberger and Utzschneider (2015), 23.
45. William Nelson and Robert W. Gordon, "An Exchange on Critical Legal Studies Between Robert W. Gordon and William Nelson," *Law and History Review*, Vol. 6, No. 1 (1988): 181.
46. See Tushnet (1991).

47. Gordon (1987), 197.
48. Allan C. Hutchinson, ed., *Critical Legal Studies* (Totowa, NJ: Rowman & Littlefield, 1989): 1.
49. Austin (1998), 10.
50. Kunal Parker, "Aftermath and Legacies," *Critical Legal Studies: Intellectual History and the History of the Present*, February, 28, 2020, Princeton, NJ; Kennedy (2006); Robert W. Gordon, "Critical Legal Histories," *Stanford Law Review*, Vol. 36, No. 1–2 (1984); Robert W. Gordon, "Historicism in Legal Scholarship," *Yale Law Journal*, Vol. 90 (1981); Morton J. Horwitz, *The Transformation of American Law, 1780–1860* (Cambridge, MA: Harvard University Press, 1977); Morton J. Horwitz, *The Transformation of American Law, 1870–1960: The Crisis of Legal Orthodoxy* (New York: Oxford University Press, 1992); Hendrik Hartog, "Pigs and Positivism," *Wisconsin Law Review*, Vol. 1985 (1985).
51. Karl E. Klare, "Theoretical Appendix," *Policy in the Nineties: A Crit Networks Conference*, Harvard Law School and Northeastern Law School, Cambridge & Boston, MA, April 11, 1992.
52. Ibid.
53. Unger (2015), 30. Gordon explains how Crits' deviationist doctrine was meant to point out how "in every corner of the legal world that you look at carefully, you'll find multiple and conflicting principles competing for recognition and dominance; and that any sense of closure legal actors feel about the system derives from their success in suppressing its immanent alternatives. Exactly the same analysis explains how CLS writers often do put forward constructive alternatives to the status quo: the alternatives are developed out of the suppressed poles of principle, policy, and social vision" Gordon (1996), 2240.
54. Unger (2015), 30–31; Duncan Kennedy, "Psycho-Social CLS: A Comment on the Cardozo Symposium," *Cardozo Law Review*, Vol. 6, No. 4 (1985): 1014.
55. See Klare (1978); Karl Klare, "Teaching *Local 1330*—Reflections on Critical Legal Pedagogy," *Unbound: Harvard Journal of the Legal Left*, Vol. 7 (2011); Freeman (1978); Gary Peller, "Race Consciousness," *Duke Law Journal*, Vol. 39, No. 4 (1990); Alan D. Freeman, "Race and Class: The Dilemma of Liberal Reform," *Yale Law Journal*, Vol. 90, No. 8 (1981); Gabel and Harris (1983); Kennedy and Gabel (1984); Duncan Kennedy, "Legal Education and the Reproduction of Hierarchy," *Journal of Legal Education*, Vol. 32, No. 4 (1982): 598.
56. Duncan Kennedy, Letter to Victor Rabinowitz, November 9, 1981.
57. "Nearly every subject area in the law school curriculum and every doctrinal field has been subject to a revaluation from a critical legal perspective" Bauman (2002), 173.

58. Mark G. Kelman, "Trashing," *Stanford Law Review*, Vol. 36, No. 1–2 (1984): 322, 325; Mark V. Tushnet, "Dia-Tribe," *Michigan Law Review*, Vol. 78, No. 5 (1980).

59. Alan David Freeman and John Henry Schlegel, "Sex, Power, and Silliness: An Essay on Ackerman's *Reconstructing American Law*," *Cardozo Law Review*, Vol. 6, No. 4 (1985); Allan C. Hutchinson, "Indiana Dworkin and Law's Empire," *Yale Law Journal*, Vol. 96, No. 3 (1987).

60. Freeman and Schlegel (1985), 847–48.

61. John H. Schlegel, Letter to David Trubek, June 14, 1977: 1.

62. Conference Program, Third Annual Conference on Critical Legal Studies, New College of California, San Francisco, CA, November 9–11, 1979.

63. For good examples of this commitment, see "2.5 *Reptile* 1," in *CLS: Newsletter of the Conference on Critical Legal Studies*, eds. Betty Mensch, Alan Freeman, and David Fraser (May 1987): 5; Peter Gabel, Letter to Morton Horwitz, March 10, 1986.

64. Kelman (1984), 326 and Kennedy and Gabel (1984), 50.

65. Feinman and Feldman (1985), 875, 877.

66. Gary Peller, "The True Left," *Unbound: Harvard Journal of the Legal Left*, Vol. 10 (2015): 105.

67. Kennedy (1984), 1–2.

68. See, e.g., "Politicizing First Year Law Teaching: Work in Progress," Discussion Group Materials, Third Annual Conference on Critical Legal Studies, New College of California, San Francisco, CA, November 11, 1979.

69. Conference Program, Fourth National Conference on Critical Legal Studies, University at Buffalo School of Law, Buffalo, NY, May 30–June 1, 1980: 3. Another good example is the Fifth Annual Conference on Critical Legal Studies, University of Minnesota Law School, Minneapolis, MN, May 15–17, 1981.

70. Conference Program, Seventh National Conference on Critical Legal Studies, Rutgers Law School, Camden, NJ, April 15–17, 1983.

71. *CLS: Newsletter of the Conference on Critical Legal Studies*, eds. Alan Freeman and Betty Mensch (November 1989): 86–95.

72. David Kairys, "Law and Politics," *George Washington Law Review*, Vol. 52, No. 2 (1984): 244.

73. Jay Feinman, Letter to Duncan Kennedy and Richard Abel, October 12, 1979. Another Crit pointed out, "Much can be done by exploiting one's position of advantage as a first-year law teacher. Once you show them that you can do law as well or better than their other teachers, they will all take you seriously. It is then possible to develop yourself for them into a locus of opposition to the rest of the faculty, personally, stylistically, and, ultimately, intellectually." Alan Freeman, Letter to Rick Abel and

Duncan Kennedy, "For: Conference on Critical Legal Studies Session on Politicizing First-Year Teaching," October 24, 1979.

74. Gordon (1989), 76–77, 82–83. Also see "Key Ideas," *Critical Legal Studies: Intellectual History and the History of the Present*, February, 28, 2020, Princeton, NJ; Boyle (1984), 10; Jay M. Feinman, "The Failure of Legal Education and the Promise of Critical Legal Studies," *Cardozo Law Review*, Vol. 6, No. 4 (1985).

75. I am thankful to Jeremy Paul for offering this important insight.

76. In "The Failure of Legal Education and the Promise of Critical Legal Studies," Jay Feinman stressed the importance of choice to critical legal teaching: "In Critical teaching, the meaning of legal doctrine is never the ostensible justification and structure. Critical teaching in a doctrine-focused course aims to expose underlying layers of meaning, rendering doctrine indeterminate. That indeterminacy provides the student with the necessity and opportunity of choice—moral, political, and professional. Faced with that choice, students must construct their own meaning of law. The Critical teacher's role is to help students understand the possibility of choice, to empower them to choose, and to offer them the teacher's own choice as a guide." Feinman (1985), 758.

77. Klare (2011), 77–78.

78. Gary Peller, "The Experience of CLS: Communities, Controversies, Reactions," *Critical Legal Studies: Intellectual History and the History of the Present*, February, 28, 2020, Princeton, NJ.

79. Kennedy (2004), 30–48, 63–65.

80. Frances Olsen, "Politics Without A Movement," *Cardozo Law Review*, Vol. 22, No. 3–4 (2001): 1111.

81. Kennedy (2014), 588; Austin (1998), 9, 22 and Boyle (1984), 18.

82. See Rand Rosenblatt and David Kairys, Letter to Frank Munger and Carroll Seron, February 23, 1983; Christopher S. Canning, Letter to Mark Tushnet, February 1, 1988; Boyle (1984), 18, 29.

83. Lucie White, Letter to Karl Klare, 1979.

84. Ibid.

85. Minda (1997), 8.

86. Kennedy (1980a), 56.

87. See, e.g., Kennedy (2014), 585, 589; Krever, Lisberger and Utzschneider (2015), 12–13; Kennedy (1985) and Duncan Kennedy (2004), 123–35.

88. Krever, Lisberger and Utzschneider (2015), 13.

89. Kelman (1984), 326.

90. "Discussion Document for Saturday Morning Plenary: Do the Critical Legal Theory Networks Have a Politics?" *Policy in the Nineties: A Crit Networks Conference*, Harvard Law School and Northeastern Law School, Cambridge & Boston, MA, April 10–12, 1992.

91. Kennedy (2004), 137.

92. See, e.g., Rand E. Rosenblatt, Letter to Critical Legal Studies Organizing Committee, Summer Campers, and other interested People, September 8, 1982; Feinman and Feldman (1985), 925.

93. Mark Tushnet, Outline for Dean of Georgetown University Law Center Application, April 25, 1988. Although Tushnet never became Dean of Georgetown Law, the Crits were able to push through substantial curricular changes at the law school, most notably the creation of the Plan B curricular track. Crits lobbied for similar reforms at schools such as University at *Buffalo School* of *Law*.

94. Kennedy and Gabel (1984), 9.

95. See, e.g., Richard L. Abel, "Socializing the Legal Profession: Can Redistributing Lawyers' Services Achieve Social Justice?" *Law & Policy*, Vol. 1, No. 1 (1979); Richard L. Abel, "A Socialist Approach to Risk," *Maryland Law Review*, Vol. 41, No. 4 (1982); Roberto Mangabeira Unger, *Politics: A Work in Constructive Social Theory* (Cambridge, UK: Cambridge University Press, 1987); Duncan Kennedy, "Rebels from Principle: Changing the Corporate Law Firm from Within," *Harvard Law School Bulletin*, Vol. 33 (Fall 1981); Karl E. Klare, "Workplace Democracy & Market Reconstruction: An Agenda for Legal Reform," *Catholic University Law Review*, Vol. 38, No. 1 (1989); William H. Simon, "Visions of Practice in Legal Thought," *Stanford Law Review*, Vol. 36, No. 1–2 (1984); Gabel and Harris (1983).

96. Tushnet (1991), 1539.

CHAPTER 4

Towards Influence and Institutionalization

Abstract This chapter highlights the meteoric rise of the CLS movement during the first half of the 1980s. Far from being a period of conservatization in the American legal academy, these years were defined by CLS growth and the Crits' drive for further influence and institutionalization.

Keywords Critical legal studies · Fem-Crits · Retrenchment · Law schools · Law professors · Conservatism

In the late 1970s, the CLS movement began its struggle to retrench the American legal academy and shift the legal consciousness of current and future legal professionals. During these early years, the Crits initiated a broad political program aimed at removing the dominant ideas, personnel, and structural powers that undergirded the legal academy. As the 1980s began, there was no letting up.

In 1980, one of the ringleaders of CLS—Duncan Kennedy—penned "Notes of an Oppositionist in Academic Politics," a straightforward call to arms that outlined how to successfully pressure your law school colleagues and reconfigure the legal academy.[1] Described in *The New Yorker* as the most read piece of Professor Kennedy's corpus, "Notes" clearly maps Crit strategies for growing their movement and retrenching the nation's

© The Author(s), under exclusive license to Springer Nature Switzerland AG 2021
P. Baumgardner, *Critical Legal Studies and the Campaign for American Law Schools,*
https://doi.org/10.1007/978-3-030-82378-8_4

law schools.[2] For example, "Notes" includes plans of action for arm-twisting peers, passing faculty petitions and academic reforms, establishing solidarity on the Left, maintaining movement discipline, facilitating ideological conversion, making strategic use of political centrists, and speaking up as a minority bloc within your professional environment.[3] Although it was inevitable that there would be law professors who disagreed with the aims of CLS, Kennedy was confident at the beginning of the decade that Crits' "off-the-wall" views could grow a broad coalition and might one day exert a stable influence over the legal academy.[4] The movement's effective mobilization promised "to exercise a dominant influence within the institution. That's when the fun begins."[5]

From this perspective, the first half of the 1980s certainly must have been quite fun for CLS. During these years, leftist law professors and students were "coming out of the closet in real numbers" and supporting the legal movement.[6] As two law professors noted in 1984, the movement was rapidly growing in size and influence: "Its sixth annual conference at Harvard in the spring of 1982 attracted an audience of almost one thousand. Articles and notes with a Critical flavor are fast becoming a regular feature of many law reviews. The influence of CLS is percolating through all levels of American law schools, from the New College of California to Harvard Law School."[7]

CLS became not just the movement du jour but the *only* real movement available for leftist legal scholars and law students who wanted to retrench American law schools and the broader legal system. According to one Crit, "There was, simply, no place else to go if you took both material and ideological analysis seriously, identified as left progressive, and worked at a law school. CLS was it."[8] The quick explosion of movement forces and the sheer number of Crits and Crit sympathizers existing by 1985 were astounding developments within the legal academy (although they have attracted no attention within political science). Multi-week summer camps were attracting up to 100 Crits and larger CLS meetings were boasting upwards of 1,000 attendees by 1985.[9] A year later, law professor Calvin Woodard wrote in the *New York Times* that the number of CLS followers was "very likely in the thousands."[10]

THE FEM-CRITS

The growing community of Crits included diverse legal thinkers and activists. For example, feminist critical legal scholars—or "Fem-Crits"—rose in strength and numbers in the legal academy during the 1980s.[11] A distinguished group of legal scholars, the Fem-Crits played a significant, yet underexplored, part in the CLS movement and in American law schools. So who exactly were the Fem-Crits? "Fem-crits began in 1982–1983 as a feminist caucus within Critical Legal Studies," one Fem-Crit has noted.[12] Although second-wave feminism and feminist legal scholarship played important roles across American colleges and universities during the 1970s and 1980s, Fem-Crits represent the select group of scholars who worked to integrate critical legal theory and feminist theory within the CLS movement.[13]

The Fem-Crits played a foundational role in the rapidly expanding CLS movement. Fem-Crits represented a core component of CLS and worked across the 1980s to build up the movement, contribute to the collectivity's various theoretical currents, and articulate new leftist practices for legal scholars and practicing attorneys.[14] Numerous Crits pointed to the "explosive growth of a serious feminist presence in the group" and praised Fem-Crit theorizing and feminist activism as significant influences on CLS.[15] Fem-Crits railed against the poor pedagogical mission of law schools, the male-centered and status quo-enforcing classroom environment, and the feigned neutrality and depoliticization of legal scholarship. According to one Fem-Crit, the group worked "to develop theories about law and subordination and the role of law in eliminating or aggravating inequalities... based on feminist legal work and on the larger feminist challenges to knowledge offered by women's studies scholarship."[16] Fem-Crits relied on their own experiences as lawyers and activists to demonstrate how legal discourse and new forms of legal reasoning could assist movement struggles and advance "a radical redefinition of social and economic responsibility and a restructuring of work and family which would transform the lives of women, particularly the many women who live in poverty."[17]

One of the most important CLS events of the decade was the 1985 annual conference—the CLS Feminist Conference. Organized by Fem-Crits Clare Dalton, Mary Joe Frug, Judi Greenberg, and Martha Minow, the CLS Feminist Conference comprised more than a singular date or planned meeting. Beginning in 1984, "regional collectives" based out of New York, Massachusetts, California, and Washington, D.C., got to work constructing the Conference.[18] This included setting up "a national network of reading groups" to get Crits across the country talking about a core set of readings and feminist ideas.[19] In a letter to fellow Crits, the CLS Feminist Conference organizers explained: "Our sense is that for the Conference to be feminist in process as well as substance it must be, at a minimum, inclusive, decentralized and participatory. Our planning strategy is to seek among the friends of the Conference for those who are willing to work together over the months ahead to explore what feminism means to them and could mean to the Conference at large."[20]

The Conference itself took place from May 31st to June 2nd at Pine Manor College in Chestnut Hill, Massachusetts. The Conference was a hit, pulling together a broad range of reading materials, small group meetings, large group discussions, workshops, paper sessions, and a movie selected by the Fem-Crit organizers. The three overarching themes of the Conference were Feminist Methodologies: Reading Cases as Feminists; Exploring Otherness: Racism and Sexism; and Exploring Otherness: Sameness and Difference in Context. Group discussions were organized around these themes, such as "Reconstructing Sexual Equality," which was led by Chris Littleton, Fran Olsen, and Carrie Menkel-Meadow ("Sex differences are problematic because they make such a difference socially. What would happen if they were costless?"). Liz Schneider, Isabel Marcus, and Rhonda Copelon led a group discussion titled "Victimization" ("The conception of women as victims underlies some legal strategies to deal with women's inequality. This group will deal with the risks and possibilities of this conception"). Other group discussions and workshops during the three days of the CLS Feminist Conference included a "Gender Variances in Identity Formation and Their Implications for Theories of Justice and Rights" group discussion led by Sarah Salter, a "Sexism in Law School Casebooks" workshop led by Nancy Erickson and Mary Joe Frug, and a "Large Firm Lawyering—Women and Hierarchy" workshop led by Judith Auerbach and Margaret Fearey.[21]

Behind the scenes, Fem-Crits consciously shaped the Conference in a way that modeled their visions of healthy professional spaces and social gatherings. As one Conference organizer (Martha Minow) described the efforts of another organizer (Mary Joe Frug):

> As Mary Joe envisioned that conference, the boundaries between work and family themselves would be remade; the conference not only provided child

care and accommodations well-suited for families. It also used the idea of families to welcome participants into assigned groups that met periodically throughout the days to help provide continuity during a potentially disorientating time.[22]

During an era that witnessed the rise of the modern Right and the creation of new conservative retrenchment efforts, the CLS Feminist Conference in 1985 stood for more than just a weekend vacation among academic colleagues. The Fem-Crits crafted the Conference in a manner representative of their broader impact on CLS. They linked disparate members together through reading, writing, and speaking opportunities, while also organizing important movement events that engaged with feminist critical legal scholarship and put forward concrete plans for a leftist future in the American legal system.

Outside of the Conference, the Fem-Crits worked tirelessly to ensure that the CLS movement would continue to retrench the legal academy. Fem-Crits pushed legal scholars to engage with the study of women's position in the law, and these critical theorists advocated for a distinctive role of women and feminist thought in reconstructed law schools. In the words of one Fem-Crit, "Feminist educators seek to question traditional notions of authority in the classroom by sharing leadership in the classroom, replacing competition with an atmosphere of trust and cooperation, integrating affective and intellectual learning, and by using personal experience as a valid source of knowledge."[23] Fem-Crits would have their students ponder questions such as "how can public and private obligations be recast so that society can alter legacies of constraining gender roles? How can the very idea of a private self be understood as an invention of public life? And... how can a woman's experiences inform a law professor's scholarship?"[24] The hope, at least among many Fem-Crits, was that new approaches to legal education—such as service-learning, civic engagement opportunities, and creative co-teaching methods—would open up "a greater range of voices in the classroom" and help law students to "feel connected both to each other in the learning process and to the parties in the cases."[25]

A Revolution on the Rise

The Fem-Crits' work demonstrates how the CLS movement was accomplishing more in the first part of the 1980s than merely adding to its membership numbers. In line with the hopes set out in "Notes of an Oppositionist in Academic Politics," many Crits were participating in the diverse retrenchment activities outlined in the previous chapter. Crits came to be seen as political activists, famous for their actions to transform the legal academy. As the Crit Peter Gabel recollects, in 1983 the legal movement was "hot" and was able to generate significant attention from legal professionals.[26] Crits attracted large crowds as they gave talks about CLS, with hundreds of law professors and students arriving to learn about the ballooning movement.[27] Additionally, numerous symposia were dedicated to understanding the movement in the early and mid-1980s (and even more included Crits as the chief foils to symposia topics).[28] In the introduction to the 1985 Symposium on Critical Legal Studies at Cardozo School of Law, the editors described the movement as "flourishing, and thereby transforming the broader law school community."[29] In fact, the editors claimed, the movement had "enlivened" their own law school and been wildly successful in "generating excitement and debate."[30]

In 1982, Crits worked with members of the National Lawyers Guild to publish something approaching a CLS textbook, which could offer "a progressive, critical analysis of current trends, decisions, and legal reasoning" across a wide range of legal fields.[31] Reporting on the early success of the book in March 1983, editor David Kairys detailed how 5,452 copies of the book had been sold in the first three months and that book events, reviews, radio interviews, and study groups related to the work had sprouted up across the country.[32] Kairys understood the growing academic and popular appeal of the movement's vision, and he believed that the book could aid in the organization and mobilization of likeminded people. He encouraged "Authors and Friends" of the book to "contact a reporter or editor at your local newspaper and any papers, journals, magazines or radio or TV stations at which you have contacts."[33]

By 1984, it was clear that the Crits' political activities were paying dividends. The CLS movement was starting to gain institutional standing and influence. At the 1984 AALS Annual Meeting, "[t]here was a buzz of conversations about Critical Legal Studies," one Crit remembers.[34] At the meeting, Crits leafleted and also hosted several offsite, "counterevent" discussions about the movement and its ideas for "institutional reform" and "curricular and appointments issues."[35] The event attracted hundreds.[36] Crit writings also gestured to the changes in the wind. For example, a 1984 edition of the *Lizard*—a witty and irreverent CLS publication from the period—paid careful attention to how the movement was "beginning to develop institutional power."[37] The publication ruminated about what CLS should do—and avoid doing—in the coming years.

More importantly, as the Crits were growing in number and in political activism, the legal academy looked like it was evolving alongside the movement. One Crit wrote in 1985 that it looked as if CLS was "rapidly institutionalizing itself," as more law students were being recruited and more Crits were finding jobs in the legal academy.[38] A few months later, another Crit observed that "[m]aterial from CLS is already infiltrating the materials used in the first-year curriculum" and that "continued institutionalization" and CLS staying power within the law schools seemed likely.[39] A cover story for *The New Republic* echoed these sentiments, assessing that CLS "has adherents among the tenured faculty at many of the nation's top schools, and its method of scholarship is spreading."[40]

Critical legal scholarship represents the final significant aspect of CLS expansion during the 1980s. The Crits' writings disrupted the mainstream discourses within the legal academy and also made serious inroads in the legal profession. *The New Republic* tracked this scholarly development, proclaiming that a "lawyer or judge who picks up a law review these days" would probably end up face-to-face with Crits' work.[41] Unlike more senior law professors within the academy, the younger Crits who joined law faculties in the 1980s were highly productive scholars. As one Crit professor who began teaching in the early 1980s recollects, "there were a lot of us flooding the market and also flooding the law reviews, and especially the elite law reviews. I mean, that was sort of our brand that the law student editors of Harvard and Yale and Stanford and a lot of law reviews thought our stuff was interesting, trendy, right, whatever combination."[42]

In fact, in 1984 the *Yale Law Journal* made the extraordinary decision to publish a bibliography of CLS work. Although admitting that "[l]egal bibliographies are a rarity," the editors of the journal described this particular list as a useful tool for categorizing "the vast Critical Legal Studies literature."[43] For the piece, two Crits accumulated hundreds of works from movement members, as well as pieces deemed most representative of the movement's political aims. Later evaluations of the legal movement's productivity reinforce both the qualitative and quantitative strength of Crits' scholarship.[44]

In conclusion, the fruits of CLS retrenchment efforts were visible across the American legal academy in the early 1980s, with successful recruitment and mentorship leading to expanding membership and growing CCLS attendance. Additionally, many Crits proved to be active scholars and institutionally minded professors, capable of influencing leading law schools.[45] One legal historian summarized the unparalleled strength of the CLS movement in 1984:

> [B]usiness is booming. Attendance at the annual conference reportedly has been growing; new 'converts' declare their allegiance daily; adherents increasingly occupy space in scholarly journals, citing one another's work and supporting one another's efforts. Indeed, the current danger for CLS is not that it will be overlooked or ignored, but that it will become too successful.[46]

What About the Reagan Revolution?

The Crits' rocketing power represents one of the most notable features of the American legal academy during this period, but it also is a feature that largely has been missed in the political science literature. The CLS movement was the strongest movement within the law schools during the late 1970s and first half of the 1980s. In terms of movement building, intellectual energy, personnel growth, and retrenchment gains, there simply was not a legal movement that could compete with CLS. If you were betting in 1980, 1982, or 1984, you could be forgiven for thinking that the Crits would carry the day in American legal education, the future of legal scholarship, and the next generation of lawyering. It would be leftist retrenchment that would fundamentally reshape the modern American legal academy.

Political science research into this era has focused on conservative forces such as the Federalist Society and the law-and-economics movement. But in terms of the popular modes of legal scholarship, the dominant culture at top law schools, the identities and work of leading legal scholars, and the forms of professional training and intellectual preparation being administered to the next generation of lawyers, political conservatives faced monumental hurdles in the early 1980s. For example, the Federalist Society was not established until 1982, and initial support for the right-wing organization was weak in its first few years. One of the first Federalist Society members recalls: "From the Federalist Society's standpoint, in the early 1980s you could count on, I would say, two sets of hands—you couldn't do it on one set of hands, you probably needed two sets of hands—the people in the legal academy who would have anything other than sheer and utter contempt for what the Federalist Society was trying to do."[47]

Similarly, the law-and-economics movement was not yet a force to be reckoned with in the law schools. The number of "lawyer-economists" in America clearly was growing in the early 1980s, but their advance into the academy was more andante than allegro. The movement did not yet have an influential role in shaping legal scholarship, law school teaching, or law school politics. Even lawyer-economists acknowledged the fair developments but uncertain future of the movement. In a paper prepared for a 1982 law-and-economics conference, George L. Priest declared that law-and-economics was intellectually stuck by the end of the 1970s and that now "the prominence of law and economics is almost certain to decline."[48] Describing "the number of scholars" who subscribed to the dominant, free marketeer brand of law-and-economics as having "always been very small," Priest saw a limited future for the movement. "I am convinced that law and economics will decline in conspicuousness in legal scholarship," Priest confessed.[49] Additionally, two law professors reviewed a range of law school course materials in 1983 and concluded that "the thin development of economics in teaching texts can only be taken as evidence that economic analysis of law in the classroom is more embryonic than real."[50]

The degree of difficulty that conservative and libertarian thoughts, thinkers, and movements experienced in cracking into the legal academy cannot be overstated, especially at leading law schools. A meaningful distinction existed between the conservatizing effects on other institutions and the changes brewing in the law schools during this period. Ronald Reagan was elected President of the United States in 1980, the US Department of Justice was efficiently staffed with conservative lawyers in the early 1980s, and President Reagan appointed numerous right-wing federal judges during this period. But the American legal academy did not budge as easily for conservatives.

The ballooning movement in many top law schools during the early 1980s was not associated with the antiregulatory lawyer-economists or any other conservative force. The movement where "business was booming," adherents were growing, and scholarship was spreading was

CLS, a collectivity of leftist legal scholars.[51] And the Crits weren't merely ballooning in the legal academy during the first half of the 1980s. They were actively seeking to retrench the academy. The CLS movement fought to change legal professionals' consciousness of the law through the retrenchment of the legal academy—the institution deemed most responsible for the production of legal professionals and the early education of those professionals. As one Crit noted in 1985, "the mainstream vision of legal education is itself the principal obstacle to reform. The picture we have in our heads of what law school is all about and how it should work is more important in maintaining the status quo than are the academic backgrounds of the faculty, the employment prospects of the students, or even financial considerations."[52]

As the CLS movement continued to rise, it was clear that the American legal academy was developing in a manner that was not in lockstep with other elements of the legal system. Conservative observers definitely noticed the intercurrence that had appeared between the legal academy and adjacent institutions. One *National Review* writer acknowledged: "The last few decades have been rough times for conservatives in the law schools. Oddly enough, the political success of the conservative movement in the real world has made the problem worse."[53]

NOTES

1. Duncan Kennedy, "Notes of an Oppositionist in Academic Politics," *Unpublished Talks on Law and Legal Education: 1976–1980*, December 1980.
2. Calvin Trillin, "A Reporter at Large: Harvard Law," *The New Yorker*, March 26, 1984.
3. Kennedy (1980b).
4. Ibid., 7–14.
5. Ibid., 25.
6. Schlegel (1984), 109.
7. Allan C. Hutchinson and Patrick J. Monahan, "Law, Politics, and the Critical Legal Scholars: The Unfolding Drama of American Legal Thought" *Stanford Law Review*, Vol. 36, No. 1–2 (1984): 201; Also see James R. Hackney, Jr., *Legal Intellectuals in Conversation: Reflections on the Construction of Contemporary American Legal Theory* (New York: New York University Press, 2012): 78.
8. Mari Matsuda, "Talking About Critical Legal Studies While We Are on the Short Clock of the World," *Critical Legal Studies: Intellectual History and the History of the Present*, February 28, 2020. Princeton, NJ.

9. Richard Lacayo, "Critical Legal Times at Harvard," *Time*, Vol. 126, Issue 20, November 18, 1985: 87; Hackney (2012), 77.

10. Calvin Woodard, "Toward A 'Super Liberal State'," *New York Times*, November 23, 1986. Also see Boyle (1984), 1.

11. See Baumgardner (2019b) for this introductory material on the Fem-Crits, as well as a lengthier discussion of how Fem-Crits' work fits within our current legal climate in the United States.

12. Frances Olsen, "In Memoriam: Mary Joe Frug," *Harvard Women's Law Journal*, Vol. 14 (1991): i.

13. For more on this integration, see Minda (1995); Martha T. McCluskey, "Defending and Developing Critical Feminist Theory as Law Leans Rightward," in *Transcending the Boundaries of Law: Generations of Feminism and Legal Theory*, ed. Martha Albertson Fineman (New York: Routledge, 2011).

14. In the words of one Crit: "The basic challenges of critical legal studies to conventional legal theory are feminist challenges. Law is supposed to be rational, intellectual, objective, abstract, and principles, just as men are; not irrational, emotional, subjective, contextualized and personalized, the way women are supposed to be. Critical legal studies challenges this description of law, and it displaces the hierarchy of rational over irrational, intellectual over emotional, objective over subjective, abstract over contextualized, and principled over personalized. The intellectual upheaval of critical legal studies and the dislocation caused by this upheaval opens the space necessary for women to try to reorient the profession." Boyle (1984), 28.

15. Schlegel (1984), 410; Carrie Menkel-Meadow, "Feminist Legal Theory, Critical Legal Studies, and Legal Education or 'The Fem-Crits Go to Law School'," *Journal of Legal Education*, Vol. 38, No. 1–2 (1988); Gordon, Interview; Tushnet (1991); Mari Matsuda, "Opening Address," *CLS: Newsletter of the Conference on Critical Legal Studies*, eds. Alan Freeman and Betty Mensch (November 1989): 64.

16. Menkel-Meadow (1988): 63; Frances Olsen, "The Family and the Market: A Study of Ideology and Legal Reform," *Harvard Law Review*, Vol. 96, No. 7 (1983); Mary Joe Frug, "Re-Reading Contracts: A Feminist Analysis of a Contracts Casebook," *American University Law Review*, Vol. 34 (1985); Clare Dalton, "An Essay in the Deconstruction of Contract Doctrine," *Yale Law Journal*, Vol. 94, No. 5 (1985); Elizabeth Schneider, "The Dialectic of Rights and Politics: Perspectives from the Women's Movement," *New York University Law Review*, Vol. 61, No. 4 (1986).

17. Schneider (1986), 650–51.

18. Menkel-Meadow (1988), 65.

19. Olsen (1991), I and Boyle (1984), 29.

20. Martha Minow, Mary Joe Frug, Judi Greenberg, and Clare Dalton, Letter to Critical Community, October 10, 1984.
21. Conference Program, CLS Feminist Conference, Pine Manor College, Chestnut Hill, MA, May 31–June 2, 1985.
22. Martha Minow, "Mary Joe and the Public Interest," *Newsletter of the Conference on Critical Legal Studies* (November 1991): 6–7.
23. Menkel-Meadow (1988), 79–80.
24. Minow (1991), 6–7.
25. Menkel-Meadow (1988), 79.
26. Peter Gabel, "The Spiritual Foundation of Attachment to Hierarchy," in *Legal Education and the Reproduction of Hierarchy: A Polemic Against the System* (New York and London: New York University Press, 2004): 154.
27. See, e.g., Brad Hudson, "Horwitz: A Critical Look at Studying Law," *Harvard Law Record*, November 19, 1982; Christie (1982).
28. See, e.g., "Symposium on Legal Scholarship: Its Nature and Purposes," *Yale Law Journal*, Vol. 90, No. 5 (1981); "Critical Legal Studies Symposium," *Stanford Law Review*, Vol. 36, No. 1–2 (1984); "Professing Law: A Colloquy on Critical Legal Studies," *St. Louis University Law Journal*, Vol. 31, No. 1 (1986); Symposium on Critical Legal Studies, *Cardozo Law Review*, Vol. 6, No. 4 (1985); Symposium on Rights, *Texas Law Review*, Vol. 62, No. 8 (1984); "Constitutional Law from a Critical Legal Perspective: A Symposium," *Buffalo Law Review*, Vol. 36, No. 2 (1987); "Symposium: Roberto Unger's *Politics: A Work in Constructive Social Theory*," *Northwestern University Law Review*, Vol. 81, No. 4 (1987); "The Public/Private Distinction," *University of Pennsylvania Law Review*, Vol. 130, No. 6 (1982); "A Symposium of Critical Legal Study," *American University Law Review*, Vol. 34, No. 4 (1985); Mark Tushnet, "Critical Legal Studies: An Introduction to Its Origins and Underpinnings," *Journal of Legal Education*, Vol. 36, No. 4 (December 1986): 515–16.
29. "Introduction," Symposium on Critical Legal Studies, *Cardozo Law Review*, Vol. 6, No. 4 (1985): 691.
30. Ibid.
31. Kairys (1998), 16.
32. David Kairys, "Report to Authors and Friends of the Politics of Law," March 1983: 1.
33. Ibid., 2.
34. Gary Minda, "Remembering the Eighties: The *Lizard* Goes to the AALS," UMKC Law Review, Vol. 75, No. 4 (2007): 1161.
35. Ibid; Peller (2015): 101–109; Conference Program, "The Politics of Legal Education," Bellevue Hotel, San Francisco, CA, January 6, 1984.
36. Minda (2007), 1166.

37. Peter Goodrich, "Satirical Legal Studies: From the Legists to the Lizard," *Michigan Law Review*, Vol. 103, No. 3 (2004): 463; *Lizard*, ed. Duncan Kennedy, No. 2, San Francisco, CA, January 6, 1984: 1, 6; Peller (2015).
38. Kennedy (1985), 1013.
39. Tushnet (1986): 505, 515–16.
40. Louis Menand, "Radicalism for Yuppies," *The New Republic*, Vol. 194, Issue 11, March 17, 1986: 21.
41. Ibid.
42. Richard Michael Fischl, Interview with Author.
43. Duncan Kennedy and Karl E. Klare, "A Bibliography of Critical Legal Studies," *Yale Law Journal*, Vol. 94, No. 2 (1984): 461.
44. See, e.g., Hutchinson (1989), 1; Fred R. Shapiro, "The Most-Cited Law Review Articles Revisited," *Chicago-Kent Law Review*, Vol. 71, No. 3 (1996).
45. Taking stock of the growing success of the movement, one *Lizard* article declared: "The networks for recruiting new people and for placing people in teaching jobs have grown apace. The number of schools at which there is something that might be called a CLS group has increased to seven: Buffalo, Georgetown, Harvard, Miami, Rutgers-C, Stanford and Wisconsin." "Inside Dope About Critical Legal Studies," *Lizard*, No. 2, ed. Duncan Kennedy, San Francisco, CA, January 6, 1984: 5. Also see Richard Michael Fischl, "Some Realism About Critical Legal Studies," *University of Miami Law Review*, Vol. 41, No. 3 (1987): 506.
46. White (1984), 649.
47. Gary Lawson, Interview with Author. Also see Paul Baumgardner, "Originalism and the Academy in Exile," *Law and History Review*, Vol. 37, No. 3 (2019).
48. George L. Priest, "The Rise of Law and Economics: A Memoir of the Early Years," in *The Origins of Law and Economics: Essays by the Founding Fathers*, eds. Francesco Parisi and Charles Kershaw Rowley (Cheltenham, UK: Edward Elgar): 351.
49. Ibid., 374, 376.
50. Ernest Gellhorn and Glen O. Robinson, "The Role of Economic Analysis in Legal Education," *Journal of Legal Education*, Vol. 33, No. 2 (1983): 268.
51. White (1984), 649.
52. Jay M. Feinman, "Reforming and Transforming," *New York Law School Law Review*, Vol. 30, No. 3 (1985): 630.
53. Charles Bork, "Battle for the Law Schools," *National Review*, September 26, 1986: 44.

CHAPTER 5

Retrenchment Repelled

Abstract The manner in which the legal academy—and adjacent institutions interested in the changes brewing within the legal academy—reacted to the CLS retrenchment project had enormous consequences for the CLS movement. This chapter illustrates the remarkable backlash that took place against the ascendant CLS movement beginning in the mid-1980s.

Keywords Critical legal studies · Retrenchment · Law schools · Law professors · The media

Law schools' reception of the second wave of Crits—"the children of the Crits"—in the second half of the 1980s would be immensely consequential, for the success or failure of this wave would have serious ramifications for the CLS movement and for the future of the American legal academy.[1] In order for the legal academy to be retrenched, this new generation of Crits would have to expand the movement's political actions and reach more law schools. Movement leaders maintained the ambition that "[w]e can win over lots of liberals. We can radicalize a lot of liberal law professors, because we have an analysis of law that is incredibly convincing for law professors...that is going to win people away from the liberals to us, and then away from the conservatives to be more liberal. So that's plausible. That could happen."[2]

But although the CLS movement had gained influence and institutional power during the early 1980s, the Crits' retrenchment campaign began to meet serious resistance during the middle of the decade. A picture of CLS arose—not just in the legal academy, but also outside in the broader public arena—that the movement represented a strong force. The Crits were not written off as a small bunch of radical intellectuals, congregating and navel-gazing at the fringes of American law. Instead, non-adherents understood CLS as posing a real, collective political threat by the mid-1980s. The early success of the Crits' retrenchment project attracted the attention of a diverse cast of actors—law school administrators, university alumni networks, lawyers, politicians, the media, and conservative organizations—that strove to contain and then marginalize CLS.

But would these reactionaries succeed? Or would their attacks merely slow the pace of CLS retrenchment? In 1985, one Crit prognosticated:

> It is not at all likely that cls will cease to exist, as a movement or as a universe of discourse, at any time in the near future. We are already far too thoroughly institutionalized for that. But cls has become sufficiently threatening (at last) to the mainstream so that we can expect a whole variety of efforts to contain or roll it back. There is nothing to say these efforts will fail. And there is no reason to believe that the outcome will be clear any time soon. The prospect is for protracted pushing and shoving.[3]

THE MEDIA AND EXPANDING THE ZONE OF CONFLICT

One particular political development that had a profound effect on the Crits' fate relates to the zone of conflict. Increasingly by the mid-1980s, the media brought negative attention to the CLS movement. Local and national media spotlighted different schools witnessing CLS activism and educational disputes; the *New York Times, Wall Street Journal, Los Angeles Times, Washington Post, New Yorker, Boston Globe, National Review,* and dozens of other media outlets reported on CLS as a subversive movement with its eyes on the legal academy.[4] Crit Peter Gabel recalls how this media attention contributed to "a public awareness that there was some radical challenge to the law that had not taken place before that was cause for alarm."[5] According to one legal historian, "no successor left-wing approach has come close to critical legal studies in capturing the attention and drawing the response of everyone else, including scholars outside law schools and even a public audience outside academia altogether."[6]

In some respects, this media crescendo would not have been out of the ordinary in the context of the Cold War, when average Americans were willing to go to great lengths to ward off anything smacking of radical leftism. As political scientist Michael Paul Rogin pointed out during the period, understanding Reaganism requires an appreciation for the "countersubversive imagination" in Cold War America and a grasp of the ubiquitous institutional efforts to weed out "subversives."[7] The scope and fervency of attacks against CLS were noteworthy examples. Even President Reagan and acting government officials went out of their way to warn lawyers and laypersons alike about the Crit threat.[8]

THE PROFESSIONAL EXPECTATIONS AND SELF-UNDERSTANDINGS CULTIVATED AMONG LAW PROFESSORS, OR: THE DEFENSE OF FAITH, MANNERS, AND PROFESSIONALISM

To better appreciate how this public awareness shaped the law schools' perception and treatment of CLS from the mid-1980s onward, we must consider several of the relevant professional expectations and self-understandings that were cultivated among legal academics and which governed law school culture during this period.[9] These expectations and self-understandings included those beliefs about professional identity and behavior, intellectual standards, and academic status that were deemed essential to the integrity, distinction, and preservation of law schools and legal academics, but which were seen as under attack by the mid-1980s. Engagement with these professional expectations and self-understandings may help to clarify why law school inhabitants fought so hard to resist the CLS movement's retrenchment project.

The dominant ideas about law professors' right relation to the law and right relation to fellow professors were communicated clearly and frequently throughout the 1980s. Law deans and law professors from the period produced a prolific amount of material explicating these professional expectations and cultivating specific self-understandings within the professoriate. For starters, many professors who were unaffiliated with CLS expressed the view that their profession demanded of them a right relation to the law while in the presence of, and instruction of, law students. Professors ought to demonstrate a degree of faith in the legal system and work to maintain the distinguished status of law. This meant, among other things, inculcating respect for the legal system and legitimating for students the diverse manifestations and impacts of laws; modern American legal institutions and practices were to be understood as fully capable of ensuring order, achieving justice, protecting rights, and furthering rational political change.[10]

Justifying and revering the transcendent character of the law required the embrace of a very particular legal consciousness and concomitant professional identity. For instance, in 1985, a Harvard Law School professor wrote about his profession: "If there is any group of lawyers who ought to be committed to the proposition that the life of the law is reason and that governance of affairs by reason is a meaningful enterprise, it certainly ought to be those whose personal vocation is to a life of thinking."[11] A few months before, a University at Buffalo School of Law professor explained in the *Journal of Legal Education* how professors' "deep cultural commitment to the ideology of the rule of law" and beliefs in the rationality, fixedness, neutrality, rule-guidedness, and justifiability of American law had become a central part of their professional identities.[12] Deans too were reminded that legal professionals have every reason to enjoy faith in contemporary legal reasoning, legal methods, and the legal system itself. There was no need to doubt that the law matters, that legal rules dictate results, or that the law holds out the promise of certainty and predictability.[13]

Returning to the realm of legal instruction, powerful understandings existed within American law schools that professors owed it to their students to teach in such a manner that enhanced students' "professional development," assimilated them into the legal profession, and prepared them for successful legal practice. Of course, preparation for successful legal practice oftentimes meant preparing students for a particular sort of professional trajectory. Writing in the *Journal of Legal Education*, one law professor described how success was presented to students:

> [T]he dominant image or goal, which if not explicitly offered is at least immanent in their surroundings, is that of the legal craftsman. This model or image of success is predominately that of the private practitioner; the pinnacle of success, both in terms of prestige and financial rewards, is to join one of the 'best' firms engaged in corporate practice. The goal of

training or becoming a skilled craftsman or private practitioner seems, in fact, to be the prevailing standard by which all educational activities are judged and must be justified.[14]

These instructional understandings led professors to "behave as professionals" and avoid modes of instruction that they considered to be overly ideological or normatively prescriptive. A former dean of Cornell Law School wrote about law professors' self-understandings as "technicians teaching technique in a value-neutral context."[15]

In 1985, Richard C. Maxwell—former dean of UCLA Law School and former president of the American Association of Law Schools (AALS)—elaborated on this necessarily circumscribed role.[16] Maxwell reiterated to law school alumni that modern legal education was designed for students to soak up "a body of principles, rules, and decisions," and then learn how to apply these settled objects to the professional tasks of predicting, analyzing, and peddling the law.[17] In the classroom, "questions of ends and values are a part of legal education only within a rather narrow professional framework."[18] Instilling professional duty was what passed as moral education in law school: "A faith emerges, but it is a faith in process: that the application of reason within a procedural structure governed by the general values of the Constitution will produce good long term results for society or, at least, an acceptable resolution of a current problem."[19]

Two years later, Katharine T. Bartlett—a law professor and future dean of Duke Law School—was of the same mind, adding that values-teaching in the legal academy was futile and her colleagues "should not attempt to impose our values upon students."[20] The only acceptable way for teachers to rub their values off on students seemed to be through modeling upright interpersonal behavior. Between 1985 and 1986, the American Bar Association's Commission on Professionalism held meetings, heard testimony from legal professionals, conducted interviews, and drafted a report concerning the maintenance of professionalism across the bar. The Committee's final report—"In the Spirit of Public Service: A Blueprint for the Rekindling of Lawyer Professionalism"—reminded law school deans and professors of their charge to be exemplars of professionalism for students.[21]

Professors' ideas of dutifully maintaining a vocational conveyor belt of non-partisan professional skills and case knowledge pervaded top American law schools and was visible in much of the formalized professional responsibility instruction from the period.[22] Breeding professional responsibility within law students entailed sheltering these novices from forms of legal skepticism and atheism, in order to produce lawyers who were clearheaded about the functional order and rightness of American laws and committed to staying the course in their future roles as legal professionals.[23] Law students were inculcated with a dominant view of lawyering and legal professionalism—an "ideology of advocacy"—premised on professional moral agnosticism, devotion to serving client interests, and maintaining "social stability."[24] In the middle of the 1980s, Erwin Chemerinsky reviewed "three major casebooks on professional responsibility" that he found "extensively used and therefore likely to reflect how professional responsibility often is taught."[25] The future dean of University of California, Irvine School of Law and University of California, Berkeley, School of Law discovered several commonalities among these casebooks:

> None make any attempt to encourage students to examine critically the role of the attorney in society. All assume that the attorney's highest mission is zealous representation of clients. None consider whether the attorney might have equally important obligations to individuals other than clients, often innocent third parties. All assume that it is appropriate for attorneys to act professionally in ways that they never would act outside their role of lawyer. None consider whether such role-differentiated behavior is healthy for the individual or best for society.[26]

Law professors during the period frequently voiced their shared views on how professors ought to relate to each other and to their professional environment. Legal academics and administrators spoke and wrote about the best practices for perpetuating their own professional status and authority, an agenda predicated on considerations of institutional continuity, risk aversion, and professional conservatism. Camaraderie, good manners, pedagogy that would not disrupt others' pedagogy, efficient and meritocratic processes of hiring and promotion, and assurances of a depoliticized work environment were the hallmarks of consummate professionalism.[27] Relatedly, law professors thought that the professional status and authority of professors hinged on carefully attending to scholarship standards and sharing a commitment to furnishing an intellectual output that was of immediate utility to practicing attorneys. In a high-profile report on the legal profession that gained national media attention, president of Harvard University and former dean of Harvard Law School

Derek C. Bok reiterated the chief importance of offering readily practical information and useful new tools to our legal system.[28] According to Bok, the legal academy was charged with producing (1) servants of the legal system who possessed a sense of professional duty to serve the system, and (2) easily applicable knowledge (and knowledge-bearing tools) for immediate legal use.[29]

Throughout the 1980s, top legal scholars and law school deans returned to the topic of maintaining standards for legal epistemology, methodology, and scholarship, so as to ensure "objectivity," "analytic underpinnings," "careful, methodologically rigorous thinking," and non-confrontational content.[30] As Robert C. Clark—who would become dean of Harvard Law School by the late 1980s—wrote in 1985, legal scholars needed to "appreciate or understand what it means to prove something" and aim "to achieve objective and value-neutral knowledge" about and for the legal system.[31] It is important to point out that these ideas were not limited to the realm of the old guard—senior profs bickering in the corridor about the better minds of olden days; these views were written about regularly and even shared during meetings of new law teachers.[32]

CONDEMNING THE CRITS

By 1985, an astounding degree of public attention was surrounding the nation's law schools. In addition to the heightened newspaper coverage centered around the legal academy, lawyer-economists and conservative legal scholars had gone on William F. Buckley's *Firing Line* television show to decry the far-left beliefs of law professors and to detail to viewers how these radical scholars represented "a threat to representative democracy."[33] Even U.S. Department of Justice official William Bradford Reynolds was publicly lamenting:

> As Assistant Attorney General for the Civil Rights Division, I am particularly well-positioned to feel the currents in the law schools today and to observe their effects upon lawyers and judges—and, indeed, upon the law itself. The past three years have fully confirmed my worst suspicions that much of the antidemocratic, result-oriented jurisprudence of our time can be traced directly to our system of legal education.[34]

This public attention, combined with the aforementioned professional expectations and self-understandings passing through the academy, would come to present a strong check on further CLS retrenchment efforts.

Academic discussions to understand the CLS movement and ascertain its adherents' degree of fit within the academy became prevalent. Law schools hosted symposia and forums to better evaluate if he was one of us, whether she sustained our ideas and expectations, and—most importantly—how much destruction and reconstruction the Crits heralded.[35] In print, law school professors and deans engaged in back-and-forth discussions over CLS, ranging in topic from Crits' contributions to the academy, members' attacks on the academy, and what the legal movement meant for the future of the professoriate. The *Journal of Legal Education*—the official AALS journal on legal education—featured dozens of such discussions during the 1980s.[36]

Not uncommonly, non-Crit participants in these discussions expressed fears that the swelling band of CLS radicals ran up against the profession's dominant ideas about professors' right relation to the law, to law professors, and to the legal academy. On the one hand, these expressions might have been expected from senior faculty. As one legal scholar pointed out in 1985: "On the ideational level most senior faculty, in whom much educational control is vested, develop a proprietary interest and concern about retaining most of the structure and content of legal education. It is not only a matter of tested tradition, but also of established and comfortable intellectual capacity and personal mastery and control."[37] However, the professional worries that the Crits generated seemed deeper and more existential than periodic changing-of-the-guard tensions.

According to one legal historian, "For law professors, critical legal studies placed even more at risk—their reason for being."[38] Two law professors at Rutgers University described the highly personal effects of the Crits' retrenchment project in the academy:

> Confronting a dominant consciousness is a tremendous threat not only to a curriculum or to legal theory but to the way in which people constitute their self-identities. Our professional identity and the circumstances in which we operate day-to-day constitute so much of our self-perception that a challenge to the principles supporting this identity and those circumstances strike very deeply. The traditional law professor has placed himself or herself in a social hierarchy and interacts with colleagues, students,

and others based on the dominant ideology. A challenge to that ideology threatens to overcome the professor's very way of being.[39]

Faculty disappointment and dread are discernible in several writings from the period. One Harvard Law School professor excoriated the Crits as too political (protesting too much for a more "nonhierarchical law school and society"), legally ignorant ("They are not knowledgeable, in detail, about most areas of law"), and "anti-professional: They do not care about the problems of the real world and real professionals, problems with which lawyers must deal."[40] In his coda, the distressed legal scholar turned to retaliation: "It is we who should cry for resistance."[41] Another law professor, who taught at the University of Virginia during the period, echoed this assessment, contending that the Crits instilled doubt about the proper training of new lawyers and the duties of modern legal professionals.[42] As such, "there was...a kind of inherent professional antipathy to critical legal studies just built into the structure of the law schools, which is focused on preparing young people to be lawyers."[43]

Crits were acutely aware of how dominant standards of teaching, training, scholarship, decorum, and professional utility were being marshaled within the legal academy to sideline the CLS movement. Crits such as Mark Tushnet, Duncan Kennedy, and Richard Michael Fischl wrote and spoke about how seemingly clinical and anodyne evaluations concerning professional and disciplinary standards were wielded against the Crits as an effective form of "turf protection."[44] Two Crits, Robert Gordon and William H. Simon, lambasted these standards, as well as the law school courses that disseminated them. According to Gordon and Simon, professional responsibility courses needed to amount to more than just harping on the occupational parameters set by professional associations.[45] Professional responsibility entailed more than just being a lawyer in good standing, knowing how to avoid disbarment, and publicly displaying punctiliousness. To retrench these backwards personal relations and resource arrangements within the legal academy, Crits like Gordon and Simon argued that law schools should bring the "sociology of everyday practice settings" into the classroom.[46] Law professors should end Socratic teaching, add more seminars and clinics, offer "more jurisprudence and more social theory," and—above all—"prepare our students to perceive what opportunities there may be to engage in reflective judgment and institutional reform."[47]

But the Crits' efforts met with considerable resistance. The orthodox professional expectations and self-understandings within the academy hurt CLS' advance. The movement's growth was interpreted as being at odds with the academy's "we all just need to get along" ethos and professional commitment to "defuse the politics and get back to the business of training lawyers."[48] The Crits came to be viewed as the leading partisans of the academic profession, who were adulterating the classroom and attacking normal, hardworking law professors.

In addition to the scholarly discussions and evaluations of CLS, various law professors and deans took up a more combative posture toward the leftist movement. This approach was defined by vicious ad hominem attacks and incessant fearmongering. Feeling "goaded...into being uncivil," some of the Crits' most aggressive attackers participated in loud, bar-the-gates rhetoric and grandstanding in the name of saving the American legal system from the critical menace.[49] As one law school dean explained, "[t]o ignore their efforts and their attractiveness for some is both dangerous and self-deluding."[50] And law schools did not ignore CLS retrenchment efforts. Instead, faculty and administrators went to war over CLS and the fate of the legal academy. In the words of one Crit:

> [L]egal academia today may be more openly politicized and more polarized than ever before. Although the ideological divisions are clearly reflected in scholarship, the political conflict in the nation's law schools does not consist of mere skirmishing over intellectual orientations or interests. Rather, it amounts to a struggle for (and against) power on many fronts - in faculty meetings as well as at law reviews, over admissions and appointment decisions as well as over interpretations of legal doctrine, and over the description and practice of the whole range of social relations.[51]

Robert Gordon remembers how the most unsettled professors depicted CLS as an insurgent movement trying to wreck America itself. "It really was seen as a cadre of leftwing guerrillas who were taking over a major American institution" and were threatening "a society-wide phenomenon," Gordon recalls. "Everybody feared that it would spread the way the 1968 revolt spread. People had an image of 1968, which just terrorized them." Of course, many Crits knew that their movement would cause friction. But, according to Gordon, "we did not expect that so much of the pushback would be so dishonest. We thought that people

who expressed themselves as adhering to liberal standards of civil debate—
reason, evidence, and so forth—would not be prone to such hysterical
kind of distortion and outright slander, as they were."[52]

A law school dean from the period attested that there was a general
sentiment among law professors he knew that Crits were a disruptive force
in the academy.[53] Similarly, the dean of Case Western Reserve University
School of Law wrote to law school alumni in 1986 that although "[t]he
organizational structure of a law school is a loose, collegial form depen-
dent upon good will, trust, and respect for colleagues," the Crits were
threatening to blow up that organizational structure.[54] The dean went
on to outline for alums the "insidious" and "appalling effect" of CLS on
the American legal academy:

> This foundation of trust and respect is being dangerously eroded, at
> schools where CLS has begun to take hold, because of a misuse of the
> professorial position and academic opportunity. For some, it has meant the
> opportunity to use the class as a forum for proselytizing particular ideas...
> If allowed to go unchecked, this politicizing of a law faculty can destroy
> even the greatest of law schools.[55]

One law professor and former federal appellate judge described CLS as
a "nihilistic neo-Marxist movement" determined to destroy their professional surroundings.[56] A Rutgers Law School professor referred to his
Crit colleagues as "pure bomb throwers" bent on "killing their elders."[57]
One legal scholar told a gathering of hundreds of university alumni that
the Crits were "a serious attack on the legitimacy of the institutions of
the United States."[58] Another law professor at a top law school recited
Yeats' *The Second Coming* to describe how CLS growth had damaged his
law school.[59]

Crusades against the Crits were fairly widespread during the second
half of the 1980s, and attacks had a way of multiplying. An institutional
mirroring of CLS marginalization took place across the country, as law
schools replicated the academic decisions and parroted the professional
concerns raised at other schools. One law professor at Case Western
Reserve University School of Law noticed that the political battles to
thwart second-generation Crits and deter CLS recruitment "played out
in varying degrees at every law school in the country," trickling down
from top-tier law school behaviors to lower-tier behaviors and eventually
constituting "a brute power conflict over control of legal education and

the future of the legal system."[60] These falling dominoes represented a serious change of course from the early 1980s, as Crits metamorphosed from new kids on the block to feared enemies engaged in a "battle to the death."[61] Here is how one Crit, Richard Michael Fischl, perceived this reversal:

> The surprise to me was that something that had seemed so exciting and, yes, edgy but a legitimate part of the discourse had...emerged as a villain and as a thing to be denounced. I remember these exchanges, one early on at like a labor section meeting of the AALS where the topic was Critical Legal Studies and Labor Law and these professors basically asking, 'Are you guys communists, or what?' kinds of questions...They were hostile. They were mean. I began to develop the grammar that helped me understand the idea of performativity. These were moves, rather than just discourse. And the moves were bullying. They were silencing. And that was a big surprise for an untenured professor.[62]

The involvement of university and law school alumni groups within this broadened zone of conflict also imposed pressure on law schools to sideline the CLS movement. Opponents of CLS organized debates and alumni outreach efforts to warn legal professionals of the Gotterdammerung occurring within their august alma maters. At one public debate in New York City, CLS was cast as an intellectually backwards force that was opposed to "Science [,] Technology [,] Business and commerce [,] Large, formal organizations [,] Capitalism [,] Conventional law practice and the legal profession [,]" and "Traditional legal scholarship."[63] The opprobrium continued: "I'm talking about deep-seated[,] thoroughgoing, fundamental antipathy and dislike for these seven things. Only that will get you into the club. If, like me, you find yourself basically in favor of these things like science, business, and the legal profession, then you'll have to seek some other path."[64]

During the same period, conservative groups, such as the Federalist Society, added tinder to the fire by mailing anti-CLS propaganda to their chapters and to law school alumni lists. Alumni from schools such as Harvard Law School and the University of Chicago Law School were mailed scathing materials on CLS, which described Crits as dangerous, utopian radicals laying siege to the academy.[65] These efforts proved successful. Hundreds of law school alumni began calling in and writing in, worried about the value of their degrees and the state of the legal academy if the Crits took over. Harvard Law School became so overwhelmed by angry alumni writing and calling to voice criticisms over the Crits that the school was forced to set up "a communications office to handle the grievances."[66] The law school dean then took the unusual step of writing to every Harvard Law School alum, in order to calm their nerves and ensure that alumni support did not falter.[67]

It also did not help CLS' fortunes that a new wave of law school administrators were elevated to powerful positions at several leading law schools during this period. Lawyer-economists, conservative scholars, and outspoken critics of CLS were well represented in the highest levels of administration within elite law schools by the second half of the 1980s. For example, lawyer-economist Guido Calabresi became dean of Yale Law School in 1985, and he immediately authorized fellow lawyer-economist George Priest to seek funding for what would become a law-and-economics center.[68] Derek Bok, the former dean of Harvard Law School, has remarked on how Olin Foundation money and the expensive new Center for Law and Economics provided him with a sense of relief in 1985, because it reduced alumni and faculty worries of a Crit takeover at Harvard.[69] Gerhard Casper, dean of the University of Chicago Law School until 1987, made thinly veiled rebukes of CLS while also speaking approvingly of law-and-economics, even going so far as to ponder how new federal judges would do in "integrating law and economics."[70] Thomas Jackson, dean of the University of Virginia Law School in the late 1980s, was a lawyer-economist. Robert Mundheim, dean of the University of Pennsylvania Law School from 1982 to 1989, was a founder of a law-and-economics journal and oversaw the creation of law-and-economics programming at Penn in 1986. And Paul D. Carrington—a legal scholar who was engaged in a number of heated, well-publicized fights in which he advocated for the removal of Crits from the legal academy—was dean of Duke University School of Law throughout much of the 1980s.[71]

This tornado of law professor, dean, alum, and lay forces eventually took its toll on the professional prospects of young Crits and on the potency of CLS retrenchment efforts. Deemed "troublemakers" who were harming established legal ideas, individuals, and institutions, quite a few children of the Crits had a difficult time getting hired and promoted.[72] One Crit recalls how, as a young law professor, he was worried about these growing attacks on CLS: "There were purges going on. There were deans who would forthrightly announce that there would never be a Crit on their faculty."[73] In fact, in 1987, law professor Jerry Frug uncovered several law schools—and law deans—that had openly expressed their unwillingness to tolerate a CLS presence on their campuses.[74] Such marginalization rose to the point that an AALS newsletter included "Dean Susan Praeger of the UCLA Law School...in a message written in her capacity as President of the Association of American Law Schools, express[] her concern that 'faculty members at self-proclaimed prestigious schools and more modest ones alike express determination that no Critical Legal Studies adherent will find a place on their faculty.'"[75]

"Politics, All the Way Down"

In a law review article titled "Of Law and the River," the dean of Duke University School of Law, Paul D. Carrington, argued that the legal academy was not a place for politicking professors, especially of the CLS variety. According to Dean Carrington, teachers with eyes set on "revolution" had no place in the law school. Instead, such scholars had "an ethical duty to depart the law school," because their political mission did not comport with schools' "accepted responsibility for training professionals."[76] The dean's remarks were not out of step with certain members of the academy. In fact, many law professors shared Carrington's view and extended it, holding that the CLS movement was so dangerous that it warranted direct and forceful institutional responses.

By the second half of the 1980s, a powerful narrative about CLS had taken hold, which depicted the Crits as threatening ideologues who were unnecessarily politicizing the law schools. One lawyer-economist at Yale Law School commented on how Crits had meetings, group positions, coordinated tactics, and plans for changing law schools. This was "pretty much unprecedented, and had never previously happened in law schools. CLS was vastly more politically self-conscious and organized."[77] And not only were the Crits politically self-conscious, but they were extremists. These Marxists and nihilists were poisonous teachers, who were disrespectful to other law professors, hated America and our national heritage, and were opposed to common sense and basic legal knowledge.[78] As such, the Crits needed to be stopped at all costs. "The critical legal studies movement cannot ultimately succeed," wrote one law professor, "because society cannot tolerate its victory."[79]

Resembling the midcentury McCarthyite witch-hunts for communists who lurked in the classrooms, the condemnation of CLS that took place several decades later represents an especially shameful chapter of Cold War hysteria. However, even some Crits have acknowledged that a shred of truth lay behind some of the damaging claims against the movement. CLS vigorously resisted the dominant legal consciousness of legal professionals, a consciousness that engaged with the American legal system as if it was neutral, objective, rationally ordered, determinate, and just.[80] This resistance included forceful charges against law professors and law schools that were seen as reinforcing and reproducing this deleterious legal consciousness among current and future legal professionals.

Whether through leafleting, teaching, workplace agitation, membership recruitment, or just "trying to organize your colleagues," Crits in the 1980s were "treating law schools as political places, where questions of power—race, sex, and class, yes, but, when locally understood, a myriad of other vectors on which power is exercised in law schools, including the ideology of the rule of law, the neutrality of individualism, the claims of the academic and the professional to their own ideals of neutrality, and the invisible social and cultural injunctions of enlightened academic culture—all of it might be contestable together."[81] According to Gary Peller, a Crit who began teaching at the University of Virginia School of Law in 1982, "The experience was that we were, from our podiums in front of law school classrooms as fellow competing teachers, we were fighting for the hearts and minds of the next generation of lawyers and offering different visions of what the law was about."[82]

Treating the law schools as sites for political contestation and retrenchment meant that attacks on law school administrators and fellow professors would occur. For example, Duncan Kennedy told attendees at a conference on legal teaching at New York University School of Law that "to build a radical movement...involves not simply supporting the liberal students against conservative students and conservative professors, but trying to act on them, to push them to the left."[83] In one particularly polemical piece within the *Lizard*, a Crit roundly rebuked those law professors who deemed CLS to be too political, loud, and aggressive to exact any serious changes on American law or legal education, venting:

> Your idea of 'change' is upgrading the Faculty Toilet with grant money for proving that there is poverty in America. You make a difference by doing things so reformist, so captured, so deferential to the powers that be (or maybe you <u>are</u> the powers that be), so co-opted and so god-damned

careerist that <u>of course</u> the right way to go about it is to TOADY. Your tactics just get you ingested by the system and shat out as a wimp.[84]

Throughout the 1980s, Crits proclaimed that "law is politics, all the way down" and that the CLS movement needed to engage in political struggle within the legal academy in order to begin the process of radically remaking the American legal system. But beginning in the mid-1980s, a broad contingent of law school administrators, university alumni networks, lawyers, politicians, the media, and conservative organizations pushed back against the Crits and successfully repelled the most ambitious elements of the CLS retrenchment project.[85]

NOTES

1. Fischl, Interview.
2. Kennedy, Interview.
3. Kennedy (1985), 1029.
4. See, e.g., Trillin (1984); Lincoln Caplan, "Is the Supreme Court Ready for This Kind of Free-Market Justice?" *Washington Post*, September 30, 1984; Woodard (1986); David Margolick, "The Trouble with America's Law Schools," *New York Times*, May 22, 1983; Al Kamen, "War Between Professors Pervades Harvard Law," *Washington Post*, December 21, 1985; David Brock, "Combating Those Campus Marxists," *Wall Street Journal*, December 12, 1985; Menand (1986); Editorial, "Lux et Veritas Redux?" *Wall Street Journal*, February 23, 1989; "The Veritas About Harvard," *Wall Street Journal*, September 3, 1986; Robert Clark, "In Critical Legal Studies, the West Is the Adversary," *Wall Street Journal*, February 23, 1989; William B. Lindsey, "Well-Plowed Fields," *National Review*, April 29, 1988; Bork (1986); Peter Mancusi, "The Harvard Law School Feud," *Boston Globe*, April 27, 1986; Ruth Marcus, "Ideologies Collide at Harvard Law," *Washington Post*, June 12, 1987; Ken Franckling, "Student Criticism, Debate Among Faculty Shake Harvard Law School," *Los Angeles Times*, February 22, 1987; Timothy Stanton, "Movement in Law Finds Niche at UW," *Milwaukee Sentinel*, September 28, 1987; Robert Gordon, Letter to Martin Peretz, March 21, 1986.
5. Gabel, Interview.
6. Baumgardner (2019b); Samuel Moyn, "Legal Theory Among the Ruins," in *Searching for Contemporary Legal Thought*, eds. Justin Desautels-Stein and Christopher Tomlins (Cambridge, UK and New York: Cambridge University Press, 2017): 99.

7. Michael Paul Rogin, *Ronald Reagan, the Movie: And Other Episodes in Political Demonology* (Berkeley, CA, Los Angeles and London: University of California Press, 1987).
8. Baumgardner (2019b); Paul M. Bator, "Legal Methodology and the Academy," *Harvard Journal of Law and Public Policy*, Vol. 8 (1985); Terry Eastland, "Radicals in the Law Schools," *Wall Street Journal*, January 10, 1986; Reagan (1988).
9. See Michel Foucault, *Power/Knowledge: Selected Interviews and Other Writings, 1972–1977*, ed. Colin Gordon, trans. Colin Gordon, Leo Marshall, John Mepham, and Kate Soper (New York: Pantheon Books, 1980).
10. See, e.g., Harold J. Berman, "The Crisis of Legal Education in America," *Boston College Law Review*, Vol. 26, No. 2 (1985); Stephen B. Young, "Beyond Bok: Historical Jurisprudence in Replacement of the Enlightenment Project," *Journal of Legal Education*, Vol. 35, No. 3 (1985); Steven J. Burton, "Reaffirming Legal Reasoning: The Challenge from the Left," *Journal of Legal Education*, Vol. 36, No. 3 (1986); Carrington (1984); Hutchinson and Monahan (1984), 202–3, 207–8; Carl A. Auerbach, "Legal Education and Some of Its Discontents," *Journal of Legal Education*, Vol. 34, No. 1 (1984): 58, 59, 65.
11. Bator (1985), 339.
12. Schlegel (1984). Also see Joseph William Singer, "The Player and the Cards: Nihilism and Legal Theory," *Yale Law Journal*, Vol. 94, No. 1 (1984); Philip C. Kissam, "The Decline of Law School Professionalism," *University of Pennsylvania Law Review*, Vol. 134, No. 2 (1986); John Henry Schlegel, "Langdell's Legacy or, the Case of the Empty Envelope," *Stanford Law Review*, Vol. 36, No. 6 (1984).
13. Alvin B. Rubin, "Does Law Matter? A Judge's Response to the Critical Legal Studies Movement," *Journal of Legal Education*, Vol. 37, No. 3 (1987).
14. James P. Rowles, "Toward Balancing the Goals of Legal Education," *Journal of Legal Education*, Vol. 31, No. 3–5 (1982): 389.
15. Roger C. Cramton, "Beyond the Ordinary Religion," *Journal of Legal Education*, Vol. 37, No. 4 (1987): 513.
16. Richard C. Maxwell, "Moral Values in Legal Education," *Duke Law Magazine*, Vol. 3, No. 2 (1985).
17. Ibid., 46.
18. Ibid.
19. Ibid., 47.
20. Katharine T. Bartlett, "Teaching Values: A Dilemma," *Journal of Legal Education*, Vol. 37, No. 4 (1987): 520.

21. *In the Spirit of Public Service: A Blueprint for the Rekindling of Lawyer Professionalism*, American Bar Association Commission on Professionalism (1986): 12, 19, 55.
22. Also see Margolick (1983); Kissam (1986), 253, 290, 302; Anthony D'Amato, "The Decline and Fall of Law Teaching in the Age of Student Consumerism," *Journal of Legal Education*, Vol. 37, No. 4 (1987); Richard Wasserstrom, "Legal Education and the Good Lawyer," *Journal of Legal Education*, Vol. 34, No. 2 (1984): 159; Robert B. McKay, "What Law Schools Can and Should Do and Sometimes Do," *New York Law School Law Review*, Vol. 30, No. 3 (1985): 510, 514.
23. Carrington (1984); "Paul D. Carrington to Robert W. Gordon," in Peter W. Martin, Robert W. Gordon, Paul D. Carrington, Paul Brest, Phillip E. Johnson, Louis B. Schwartz, William W. Van Alstyne, Guido Calabresi, and Owen M. Fiss, "'Of Law and the River,' and of Nihilism and Academic Freedom," *Journal of Legal Education*, Vol. 35, No. 1 (1985); Robert S. Redmount, "The Future of Legal Education: Perspective and Prescription," *New York Law School Law Review*, Vol. 30, No. 3 (1985): 562; Rowles (1982), 386.
24. William H. Simon, "The Ideology of Advocacy: Procedural Justice and Professional Ethics," *Wisconsin Law Review*, Vol. 1978 (1978): 33.
25. Erwin Chemerinsky, "Pedagogy without Purpose: An Essay on Professional Responsibility Courses and Casebooks," *American Bar Foundation Research Journal*, Vol. 10, No. 1 (1985): 189–90.
26. Ibid., 190.
27. See Hal Scott, "Legal Education: Proposals for Change," *Harvard Journal of Law and Public Policy*, Vol. 8 (1985): 318, 320; Robert W. Gordon, "Lawyers as the 'American Aristocracy,'" *Stanford Lawyer*, Vol. 20, No. 1 (1985): 81; Margolick (1983); Berman (1985); Peller (2015), 106; "Louis B. Schwartz to Paul Brest," in Peter W. Martin, Robert W. Gordon, Paul D. Carrington, Paul Brest, Phillip E. Johnson, Louis B. Schwartz, William W. Van Alstyne, Guido Calabresi, and Owen M. Fiss, "'Of Law and the River,' and of Nihilism and Academic Freedom," *Journal of Legal Education*, Vol. 35, No. 1 (1985): 19–20; Kairys (1998), 5, 15; Earl Maltz, Interview with Author; Gary Peller, Interview with Author.
28. Derek C. Bok, "A Flawed System of Law Practice and Training," *Journal of Legal Education*, Vol. 33, No. 4 (1983): 581–84; "Too Much Law—and Too Little," *New York Times*, April 23, 1983.
29. Ibid.
30. See, e.g., Mary Kay Kane, "Some Thoughts on Scholarship for Beginning Teachers," *Journal of Legal Education*, Vol. 37, No. 1 (1987); Bator (1985); David Margolick, "Legal Notes; A Professor at Harvard Law Heads to West and to Right," *New York Times*, September 15, 1985;

Owen M. Fiss, "Objectivity and Interpretation," *Stanford Law Review*, Vol. 34, No. 4 (1982); Robert C. Clark, "The Return of Langdell," *Harvard Journal of Law and Public Policy*, Vol. 8 (1985): 307.

31. Clark (1985), 301, 305, 307.

32. Kane (1987).

33. Firing Line, "How Active a Supreme Court?" *PBS*, February 10, 1980. https://digitalcollections.hoover.org/images/Collections/80040/ 80040_s0404_trans.pdf; Firing Line, "The Trouble with Lawyers," *PBS*. July 10, 1985. https://digitalcollections.hoover.org/images/Collec tions/80040/80040_s0654_trans.pdf.

34. William Bradford Reynolds, "Renewing the American Constitutional Heritage," *Harvard Journal of Law and Public Policy*, Vol. 8 (1984): 225, 228.

35. One forum from the 1984–1985 school year was aptly titled, "Do Critical Legal Studies Scholars Belong on Law School Faculties?" George W. Hicks, Jr., "The Conservative Influence of the Federalist Society on the Harvard Law School Student Body," *Harvard Journal of Law and Public Policy*, Vol. 29, No. 2 (2006): 671.

36. See, e.g., Graham Hughes, "The Great American Legal Scholarship Bazaar," *Journal of Legal Education*, Vol. 33, No. 3 (1983); Mark Kelman, "The Past and Future of Legal Scholarship," *Journal of Legal Education*, Vol. 33, No. 3 (1983); G. Edward White, "Closing the Cycle," *Journal of Legal Education*, Vol. 33, No. 3 (1983); David M. Trubek, "A Strategy for Legal Studies: Getting Bok to Work," *Journal of Legal Education*, Vol. 33, No. 4 (1983); Schlegel (1984); Carrington (1984); Martin et al. (1985); Ted Finman, "Critical Legal Studies, Professionalism, and Academic Freedom: Exploring the Tributaries of Carrington's River," *Journal of Legal Education*, Vol. 35, No. 2 (1985); Young (1985); Thomas D. Morgan, "Teaching Students for the 21st Century," *Journal of Legal Education*, Vol. 36, No. 3 (1986); Burton (1986); Tushnet (1986); Andrew L. Kaufman, "Judges or Scholars: To Whom Shall We Look for Our Constitutional Law?" *Journal of Legal Education*, Vol. 37, No. 2 (1987); Daniel H. Benson, "The You Bet Metaphorical Reconstructionalist School," *Journal of Legal Education*, Vol. 37, No. 2 (1987); Kane (1987); Aviam Soifer, "MuSings," *Journal of Legal Education*, Vol. 37, No. 1 (1987); Rubin (1987); Anthony D'Amato, "The Ultimate Critical Legal Studies Article: A Fissiparous Analysis," *Journal of Legal Education*, Vol. 37, No. 3 (1987); D'Amato (1987a); Menkel-Meadow (1988); Catharine W. Hantzis, "Kingsfield and Kennedy: Reappraising the Male Models of Law School Teaching," *Journal of Legal Education*, Vol. 38, No. 1/2 (1988); R. B. Craswell, "Some Notes on Current Trends in Legal Scholarship," *Journal of Legal Education*, Vol. 38, No. 1/2 (1988); Paul J. Spiegelman, "Integrating Doctrine, Theory and Practice in the

Law School Curriculum: The Logic of Jake's Ladder in the Context of Amy's Web," *Journal of Legal Education*, Vol. 38, No. 1–2 (1988); Robert MacCrate, "Paradigm Lost—Or Revised and Regained?" *Journal of Legal Education*, Vol. 38, No. 3 (1988); Joseph P. Tomain, "Law Students and Lawyering: Prologue," *Journal of Legal Education*, Vol. 38, No. 4 (1988); Joseph P. Tomain, "Epilogue," *Journal of Legal Education*, Vol. 38, No. 4 (1988); Richard F. Devlin, "Legal Education as Political Consciousness-Raising or Paving the Road to Hell," *Journal of Legal Education*, Vol. 39, No. 2 (1989); Peter H. Schuck, "Why Don't Law Professors Do More Empirical Research?" *Journal of Legal Education*, Vol. 39, No. 3 (1989); John S. Elson, "The Case Against Legal Scholarship or, If the Professor Must Publish, Must the Profession Perish?" *Journal of Legal Education*, Vol. 39, No. 3 (1989); Eleanor M. Fox, "The Good Law School, the Good Curriculum, and the Mind and the Heart," *Journal of Legal Education*, Vol. 39, No. 4 (1989).

37. Redmount (1985), 572.
38. Kalman (1996), 86.
39. Feinman and Feldman (1985), 929.
40. Scott (1985), 318, 320.
41. Ibid., 321.
42. Edmund Kitch, Interview with Author.
43. Ibid. Also see Kamen (1985).
44. See Richard Michael Fischl, "The Question That Killed Critical Legal Studies," *Law & Social Inquiry*, Vol. 17, No. 4 (1992): 780, 782, 802, 805; Kennedy (1985), 1029–30; "A Discussion on Critical Legal Studies at the Harvard Law School," *Harvard Society for Law & Public Policy* (1985): 21; Hutchinson and Monahan (1984): 200; Mark Tushnet, Paper for "Ideology, Competence, and Faculty Selection: Departmental Practices" Panel, *American Association of University Professors Seventy-First Annual Meeting*, Washington, DC, June 13, 1985; Nelson and Gordon (1988); David Sugarman, "Robert W. Gordon in Conversation with David Sugarman," *The Docket, Law and History Review*, Vol. 1, No. 3 (2018).
45. Robert W. Gordon and William H. Simon, "The Redemption of Professionalism?" in *Lawyers' Ideals/Lawyers' Practices: Transformations in the American Legal Profession*, eds. Robert L. Nelson, David M. Trubek, and Rayman L. Solomon (Ithaca, NY: Cornell University Press, 1992): 236–40.
46. Ibid., 238.
47. Ibid., 237, 238, 240.
48. "Lux et Veritas Redux?" (1989).
49. Trillin (1984), 59.
50. Ernest Gellhorn, "The Dean Reports," *In Brief* (May 1986): 2.

51. Gary Peller, "The Politics of Reconstruction," *Harvard Law Review*, Vol. 98, No. 4 (1985): 863.
52. Gordon, Interview.
53. Robert H. Mundheim, Interview with Author.
54. Gellhorn (1986), 1.
55. Ibid.
56. Bork (1990), 207–8, 339.
57. Maltz, Interview.
58. Harvard Society for Law & Public Policy (1985), 22.
59. Clark (1985), 299. Also see "Lux et Veritas Redux?" (1989) and Clark (1989).
60. Austin (1998), 1, 9, 22. Also see William W. Bratton, "Manners, Metaprinciples, Metapolitics and Kennedy's *Form and Substance*," *Cardozo Law Review*, Vol. 6, No. 4 (1985): 871; Fischl, Interview; Holland (1985); Hackney, Jr. (2012), 111. On the elitism of such academic phenomena, Cass Sunstein writes, "the signals sent by well-known academics, and academics at well-known schools, are likely to be especially loud... Those who are in a position to start cascades operate as leaders, above all because of the social amplification of their voices." Cass R. Sunstein, "On Academic Fads and Fashions," *Michigan Law Review*, Vol. 99, No. 6 (2001): 1260. Also see E. Gordon Gee and Donald W. Jackson, *Following the Leader? The Unexamined Consensus in Law School Curricula* (New York: Meilen Press, 1975); Wendy Nelson Espeland and Michael Sauder, *Engines of Anxiety: Academic Rankings, Reputation, and Accountability* (New York: Russell Sage Foundation, 2016); *Conference on Legal Education in the 1980s*, American Bar Association Section of Legal Education and Admission to the Bar and New York University School of Law, ed. Carrie L. Hedges (American Bar Association, 1982): 71.
61. "Lux et Veritas Redux?" (1989).
62. Fischl, Interview.
63. Hicks, Jr. (2006), 675 and Harvard Society for Law & Public Policy (1985), 6.
64. Ibid.
65. Hicks, Jr. (2006), 680–2; Mary E. Becker, "Four Faces of Liberal Legal Thought," *The University of Chicago Law School Record*, Vol. 34, No. 2 (1988): 14–16.
66. Hicks, Jr. (2006), 682.
67. Ibid; Marc Granetz, "Duncan the Doughnut," *The New Republic*, Vol. 194, Issue 11, March 17, 1986: 22; Keith Aoki, *Supplement to Casual Legal Studies: Art During Law School* (1990): 5.
68. I thank George Priest for clarifying this point, as well as offering the general timeline of Olin Foundation support to the Yale Law School.

69. Jane Mayer, *Dark Money: The Hidden History of the Billionaires Behind the Rise of the Radical Right* (New York: Doubleday, 2016): 128; John J. Miller, *A Gift of Freedom: How the John M. Olin Foundation Changed America* (San Francisco: Encounter Books, 2006): 76.
70. Gerhard Casper, "Antonin Scalia: Shades of Things to Come," *The University of Chicago Law School Record*, Vol. 32, No. 2 (1986): 20–22. Also see Steven M. Teles, "Conservative Mobilization against Entrenched Liberalism," in *The Transformation of American Politics: Activist Government and the Rise of Conservatism*, eds. Paul Pierson and Theda Skocpol (Princeton, NJ and Oxford: Princeton University Press, 2007): 179.
71. Carrington (1984) and Martin et al. (1985).
72. See, e.g., Frug (1987), 684; Hicks, Jr. (2006), 684; Jennifer A. Kingson, "Harvard Tenure Battle Puts 'Critical Legal Studies' on Trial," *New York Times*, August 30, 1987; Ad Hoc Committee on HLS to Association of American Law Schools' Committee on Academic Freedom, "Letter of Concern and Request for Inquiry Regarding Tenure Denials at Harvard Law School," June 1987; "Dear Colleague," Letter from Morton Horwitz, Gerard Clark, Aviam Soifer, Mark Brodin, Karl Klare, Wendy Parmet, and undersigned to The Board of Trustees, New England School of Law, May 11, 1987; Karl E. Klare, Letter to Edward J. Bloustein, August 14, 1984; Horwitz, Interview.
73. Fischl, Interview. Also see Mark Wittow, Letter to Jack Rosenthal, Editorial Page Editor, *New York Times*, June 15, 1987.
74. Frug (1987), 685; Gellhorn (1986), 1–2. Also see Nelson and Gordon (1988), 153–54. Gordon decried, "The head of the appointments committee of a major law school said recently that his committee would not even interview graduates of law schools with significant numbers of CLS faculty because of the risk that those graduates might have been contaminated by CLS ideas, and that hiring one might cause his school to be taken over by Them."
75. Frug (1987), 684.
76. Carrington (1984), 227.
77. Robert C. Ellickson, Interview with Author.
78. Richard A. Posner, "Bookshelf: A Manifesto for Legal Renegades," *Wall Street Journal*, January 27, 1988.
79. Scott (1985), 320.
80. See, e.g., Peter Gabel, "Dukakis's Defeat and the Transformative Possibilities of Legal Culture," *Tikkun*, Vol. 4, No. 2 (1989): 14–15, 108; Hutchinson and Monahan (1984); G. Edward White, "From Realism to Critical Legal Studies: A Truncated Intellectual History," *Southwestern Law Journal*, Vol. 40, No. 2 (1986): 835; Duncan Kennedy, "Towards Understanding the Ideological Content of a Class in Civil Procedure," *Unpublished Talks on Law and Legal Education: 1976–1980*, March 4,

1976; Singer (1984); Pierre Schlag, "Clerks in the Maze," *Michigan Law Review*, Vol. 91, No. 8 (1993); Martha Minow, "Law Turning Outward," *Telos*, No. 73 (1987).

81. Peller (2015), 104 and Peller, Interview.
82. Peller, Interview.
83. Duncan Kennedy, "Liberal Values in Legal Education," *Nova Law Journal*, Vol. 10, No. 2 (1986): 606.
84. "News of the AALS," *Lizard*, Ed. Duncan Kennedy, No. 1, San Francisco, CA, January 5, 1984: 2.
85. Tushnet (1991), 1526.

CHAPTER 6

Critical Lessons and the Campaign That Continues

Abstract This closing chapter looks beyond the 1980s and the official end of the CLS movement in order to appreciate the long-term lessons provided by the Crits. The Crits have left an indelible imprint on the modern legal academy in the United States, and they have demonstrated how leftist legal reform might emerge out of law schools today.

Keywords Critical legal studies · Law schools · Law professors · Retrenchment · Leftism

As the 1980s wound to a close, it was apparent that the American legal academy was not the same institution that it had been five years before. By 1990, the political power of the CLS movement was no longer growing within the academy. As an organized legal movement, CLS had fatally fractured by the 1990s, with fewer and fewer meetings, conferences, and opportunities for effective retrenchment of American law schools. Conservative observers outside of the academy—including the President of the United States—noticed this positive development. Speaking at the Second Annual Lawyers' Convention of the Federalist Society, Ronald Reagan connected the weakening of the CLS movement to the changing tide of American law and politics:

P. Baumgardner, *Critical Legal Studies and the Campaign for American Law Schools,* https://doi.org/10.1007/978-3-030-82378-8_6

How far we've come these last 8 years, not only in transforming the operations of government, not only in transforming the Departments and agencies and even the Federal judiciary, but also in changing the terms of national debate...To think of it, in schools where just a few years ago the critical legal studies movement stood virtually unchallenged, like some misplaced monster of prehistoric radicalism—[laughter]—today you are vexing the dogmatists of the left.[1]

Yet, despite President Reagan's triumphalism, the Crits maintained a profound influence on the law, even after the official CLS movement had faded.

Moving Beyond the 1980s

The Crits taught thousands of law students over the course of the 1980s, and they strongly influenced the next generation of leftist lawyers and legal scholars. Recently, Robert Gordon looked back and reflected, "Where CLS was most successful, I think, was as a form of local critique of conventional doctrinal and policy analysis in the law school classroom."[2] Crits' teaching and scholarship supplied students with the tools that they needed for progressive lawyering, by revealing the suppressed doctrines and principles within different legal fields and highlighting the full array of political possibilities that leftist legal professionals could exploit. Additionally, inside today's law schools, leading legal scholars have appropriated key CLS texts and arguments (even when they have not taken on board the concomitant CLS retrenchment aims).[3] According to Cheryl Harris, a legal scholar who began teaching in 1990:

In the absence of a visible CLS platform, there has been an out-migration of some of its leading proponents into other arenas and ventures, including constitutional law, political theory, law and society, legal history, international law, and the like. With some exceptions, the intellectual insights of CLS became subtext within broader legal discourses and debates.[4]

Furthermore, CLS inspired New Leftist movements both within the United States and internationally, with Crits and their students shaping international legal advocacy, critical legal theory, and the direction of legal organizations beyond the 1980s. Recall that CLS was a remarkably diverse collectivity, and Fem-Crits and critical race theorists had been growing in number by the end of the 1980s.[5] At CLS meetings, Mari Matsuda remembers how "we experienced the discomfort of intercultural communication and the politics of identity. Unlike the right-wingers who use identity as a dirty word, I believe our thinking grew sharper by asking hard questions about the collapse of the civil rights movement into liberal legalism, and the role of white supremacy in keeping capitalism on life support."[6] The CLS movement played an important role in the development of critical race theory (CRT) within the legal academy, serving as "a catalyst of CRT" and providing "a place to continue the Critical Race conversation alongside white allies."[7] The movement of critical race theorists that grew out of—and beyond—the CLS movement still exists and thrives in the United States, as do other vibrant successor movements such as the LatCrits and ClassCrits.[8]

Contemporary feminist and queer legal theory also fruitfully engage with the legacy of the CLS movement.[9] At a recent legal conference, Aziza Ahmed explained, "Despite ongoing declarations of the death of CLS, the ideas generated by CLS, it turns out, are alive and well in feminist, queer, and gender studies. Scholars are actively engaged in a project of mobilizing, grappling with, and disagreeing with core CLS claims."[10] Although the organized CLS movement may be gone, it is clear that much of the Crits' political program and powerful legal analysis has survived through a host of leftist groups in the United States. As one American legal scholar pointed out in 2020, "As I talk to young organizers on the frontlines—from Black Lives Matter to the ones taking on hedge funds—they are asking the same questions CLS asked."[11]

Surprisingly, the Crit legacy might be even stronger outside of the United States. For example, as the Cold War was ending, Karl Klare and a delegation of Crits traveled to Eastern Europe. The Crits organized a legal conference in Poland and "visited Czechoslovakia, meeting top-ranking lawyers in the new democratic government."[12] The Crits worked to build alliances with these legal professionals and to influence the fashioning of new constitutions and political arrangements in Eastern Europe. Following the trip, David Trubek expressed worry about the Europeans' "lack of any coherent post-communist modes of thinking and the tendency to revert to conservative, pre-War liberalism" and to "throw out anything associated with the communists, and thus to reinforce the most conservative forces in the society."[13] But the Crit delegation pushed back against this tendency:

I think it is fair to say that most of the people we talked to thought that there is a canonical form of market, and that this form has built in consequences for law. We exploded that myth and got some of them to see that they face a wide range of choices with profoundly different distributional and allocational consequences. In this sense, the CLS critique proved to be a useful tool.[14]

In the years that followed, Crits continued to shape public international law and the law-and-development field. Since the 1990s, CLS approaches have become increasingly popular in European and South American law schools, and Crits also have aided in the creation and work of the International Network on Transformative Employment and Labor Law (INTELL) and the International Social and Economic Rights Project (iSERP).[15] According to one of the creators of iSERP, this legal network—which addresses housing, environmental, social welfare, and various economic concerns across the globe—"should be considered in significant part a descendent of CLS," which translates CLS perspectives into international legal advocacy.[16]

These various domestic and international continuations of the CLS campaign should serve as welcome news to the American Left today. It is not uncommon for vicious assaults and bellicose exchanges to take place between Old Lefts and New Lefts. Just this past year, 81 former members of Students for a Democratic Society (SDS) published an open letter in *The Nation* chiding former Bernie Sanders supporters and American socialists for not being supportive—or supportive enough—of Joe Biden's presidential campaign.[17] Invoking the case of a divided German Left aiding in the rise of Adolf Hitler, the erstwhile SDS activists warned the "New New Left" not to make the same mistake. "Get together, beat Trump, and fight for democracy—precious, fragile, worth keeping," the letter concluded.[18] Naturally, younger socialists rebutted the sanctimoniousness of their elders and wondered how these committed radicals of yesteryear could have transformed into such cautious anti-dogmatists, Democratic loyalists who offered so little in the way of real institutional lessons and ideological support.[19]

By comparison, the Crits appear to have cultivated more dynamic and intergenerational ties, with both legal scholars and law students in the twenty-first century deriving inspiration and insight from the CLS movement. At a recent conference that reflected on the movement, scholars and students from across the United States discussed ways in which the

Crits' aims could be carried out in today's law schools.[20] In addition to the aforementioned CLS-inspired collectivities, other leftist campaigns in American law were considered. For instance, could the recently developed Law and Political Economy Project assume the Crits' mantle and grow into a leftist movement capable of achieving real structural change within the law schools and the broader legal system?[21] Or what about older associations such as the Law and Society Association? Could they be repurposed for left-wing retrenchment?

Lessons—Activist and Academic

As new generations of leftist legal professionals engage with the legacy of the CLS movement, a multitude of historical lessons, movement hurdles, and cautionary tales needs to be addressed. By uncovering the Crits' revolutionary attempts at retrenching the legal academy and breaking the liberal consensus within the American legal system, this book should assist leftists in their full accounting of the movement.

A few points, in particular, should be reclarified and recapitulated. For instance, it is important to reiterate the ways in which the Crits' campaign for American law schools did not exemplify a straightforward, marketplace-of-ideas understanding of the legal academy, the political potentiality of legal scholars, or the processes involved in academic ideas shaping institutions. Support structures deeply affected the development of the CLS movement and the fate of the movement's retrenchment efforts. The resources and allies marshaled, the zone of conflict achieved, the membership goods and professional statuses attached to the movement, the discourse and popular framing of the political conflict that ended up sticking—all of these factors heavily influenced how the Crits' political aims fared within the legal academy.[22]

The distribution of resources and uneven support for CLS certainly weakened the movement during the second half of the 1980s. The movement established a rich network of professorial support and recruited new members effectively throughout the late 1970s and early 1980s. The public attention that came to surround CLS in the 1980s and the continued local and national press focused on the Crits reflect the degree of movement power and political threat that CLS had achieved. But clear disincentives hindered recruitment and professional advancement beginning in the mid-1980s. The legal academy responded to public calls to neutralize radical teachers, and by the end of the decade, Crits were having difficulty getting hired.[23] In extreme cases, law school deans openly expressed their refusal to hire CLS members, and high-profile purges of Crits occurred at several law schools.[24] Two Crits explained why and how the CLS movement's retrenchment project was marginalized at their own law school:

> Consciousness-confronting politics makes it impossible to maintain pluralist politics-as-usual. Confronting the ideology demonstrates the political nature of the law school by showing that the institutional norms of consensus, rationality, and civility are part of the ideology, not the reality. The challenge could be met in three ways. Traditionalists could enter into the debate about fundamental issues. They could refuse to debate, but cede part of the law school to the challengers as a means of accommodation. What happened in our case, however, is that the traditionalists refused to debate and instead attempted to obliterate the challenge by force rather than by debate. Thus, appointment, promotion, and tenure decisions were politically motivated, nontraditional teaching was criticized as unprofessional, and curricular innovation of any sort was rejected as revolutionary.[25]

The CLS movement was a strong and growing legal movement by the middle of the 1980s. Crits came to be seen by many (and written about by many) as the disruptive bad boys of the academy, who were seriously threatening the stability of the American legal system. This characterization was an easy sell, based on some of the Crits' political actions and their full-throated critiques of the law school culture and their fellow professors. One Crit liked to remind his comrades, "when they find out what we're doing, they're going to come after us with guns."[26] No one ever did come after the Crits with guns. However, convinced that the CLS movement possessed a legal agenda that was too unprofessional and radically leftwing for new lawyers, large groups of professors, administrators, law school alumni, and concerned citizens did mobilize in the second half of the 1980s to weaken the powerful legal movement.

Another important lesson for present-day leftist scholars and legal activists: there is a reason that the previous chapters have said nothing about money. The CLS movement never acquired any financial resources of note, and the movement's internal structure was largely limited to the movement's Organizing Committee and the organizational foundation, the CCLS. In the early years of the movement, Crits discussed expanding movement relations, adding "more structure," and "establishing an institutional base for the organization."[27] But the Crits decided against the formation of a research center or a professional association, like the Law and Society Association, which could have offered a more formalized and extensive organizational structure, including a permanent base or executive office with staff, fundraising, strategic missions, and streamlined recruitment. David Trubek opines, "Had there been some foundation that might have given CLS $2 million, and for that insisted on a certain degree of organization, maybe that would have happened. But that wasn't in the cards."[28]

CLS was a standalone movement, largely led and membered by leftist legal scholars. For the Crits, the law school provided the perfect home base for developing intellectual capital, movement building, and starting political mobilizations. And although CLS did engage in several activities outside of the legal academy, once the zone of conflict expanded in the mid-1980s, those outside efforts were not robust enough to protect or expand the movement. Crits did not have any powerful backers or political organizations beyond the academy to connect with and sustain the struggle.

Of course, the CLS movement does not only offer lessons for new generations of left-wing legal scholars and activists. The Crits' campaign for American law schools also supplies new and essential insights for political scientists and for those who research the politics of the legal academy. Just as American society and governmental institutions were changing during the 1980s, American law schools were changing too, and law professors played a large role in these alterations. As Karen Orren and Stephen Skowronek point out in *The Search for American Political Development*, an institution participates in the developmental processes that are shaping it. An institution provides important constraints and opportunities to those actors who inhabit the institution and are (re)constructing it.[29] This principle of institutional self-participation certainly applies to legal scholars working in American law schools during the 1980s, who served as active participants in the changes that these institutions generated for themselves and for adjacent institutions.

It is encouraging that political scientists have begun grappling with legal academics and the politics of the legal academy. Legal academics are essential objects of political research, for they represent a unique class of actors within American politics. These scholars shape the hearts and minds of both lawyers and laity. In fact, there are powerful examples in

American history of legal academics exerting strong influences over the direction of the legal system.[30]

In recent years, several political scientists have researched the role of law schools and law professors in the development of the American legal system since the 1980s. Much of this political science scholarship is well-researched and of great value, and previous chapters of this book have referenced, contested, and extended conversations from the discipline. Unfortunately, almost all of these earlier studies have been captured by conservatism; they have framed the key institutional and ideological developments in the legal academy strictly in terms of conservatization (conservative totalization), and/or they have projected a fatalism onto leftist reform (left fatalism).

What are the consequences of conservative capture? An overemphasis on conservative reformers and reforms has reduced our understanding of modern American legal development to mono-causal and mono-ideological stories of conservative rollbacks of large national programs, Democratic Party-supported policies, and former liberal gains, while erasing the powerful movement mobilizations and institutional challenges that have developed on the left since the 1980s. This book has sought to challenge the common, linear retrenchment narrative of the 1980s, wherein a nebulous umbrella collectivity—the modern conservative legal movement—seamlessly achieved a single, large-scale retrenchment project across the American legal system. Unlike past studies of legal reformers and reform movements of the 1980s, the political efforts covered in this book were pioneered by leftists—members of the CLS movement—who were headquartered within American law schools.

The meteoric rise of CLS and the promise of left-wing retrenchment within the American legal academy in the 1980s undercut the supposed fait accompli of conservative reform during the decade. By framing the institutional and ideological developments occurring within the law schools solely through the prism of modern conservatism, scholars have ignored the political struggles of one of the most important legal movements of the 1980s and overlooked the hope for leftist reform that existed within American law schools and the legal profession during the period. The Crits' campaign highlights both the contested nature and direction of legal reform in the 1980s, which amounted to more than just moving backwards, moving to the right, moving to repeal liberal advances, or moving to downsize the government.

The Crits' campaign for American law schools also teaches us something valuable about retrenchment. As Sarah Staszak observed in *No Day
in Court: Access to Justice and the Politics of Judicial Retrenchment*:

> [R]etrenchment efforts are often subsumed within a pervasive narrative
> of state growth and development, or otherwise lumped into the politics
> of a single historical period dominated by the conservative legal move-
> ment. What is lost in these approaches...is that institutional change can
> take different forms over time, as reformers respond to the particular
> constellation of political and institutional barriers that they face.[31]

Even monumental regime changes do not guarantee that a uniform or
successful set of retrenchment projects will accompany the new regime.
Instead, retrenchment projects—when they do arise—look remarkably
different across various institutions. From the late 1970s through the
1980s, the hurdles that movement conservatives faced in American law
schools were quite distinct. During this period, the institutional and ideological developments within and around the legal academy were especially
turbulent and contingent. Even as conservative forces desperately sought
a foothold within the law schools, they achieved limited success for years.
Instead, it was the CLS movement's radical retrenchment project that had
the leg up within many leading law schools.

But the Crits did not achieve all that they set out to achieve, we are
reminded. The CLS movement was fatally fractured by the 1990s. That
is true. However, political scientists would be wise to still ruminate on
the value of semi-successful and unsuccessful retrenchment efforts. Such
"failings" have been tremendously consequential to the development of
ideas and institutions in American politics.[32] For example, semi-successful
and unsuccessful retrenchments have furnished the necessary material for
the formation of more successful retrenchment efforts.

By studying the dynamics of retrenchment more closely, political scientists can locate the missed political opportunities and institutional reform
possibilities across history. Semi-successful and unsuccessful retrenchers
also supply essential information about the peculiar nature of different
institutions and those who have struggled within those institutions. As
two political scientists recently noted:

> [L]earning how to lose a political contest can be as important as learning
> how to win. Traditional narratives of American politics—of victory and

loss—obscure this…conventional understandings of what it meant to win or lose prevented most observers, at the time and afterward, from seeing the opportunities that were created and sustained by the losers…Only by recognizing that the losers have agency—by seeing them not as passive and vanquished victims but as political actors with strategies of their own and capable of creating legacies of their own—can we begin to appreciate their impress on American politics.[33]

The Crits' retrenchment efforts are especially illuminating, and they reinforce the centrality of law schools within our legal system. In a 1980 report on "Law Schools and Professional Education," the American Bar Association (ABA) emphasized the long-term significance of the legal academy, stating: "By one means or another, consciously or unknowingly, law schools and the legal profession inevitably choose the sorts of graduates they wish to produce, the ethical standards and qualities they deem important, and the role they would have lawyers and the legal profession play in our society."[34] The previous chapters have reinforced the ABA's assessment, finding the legal academy to be a leading idea maker in the American legal system and an institution of intense political significance. It is because of this that mobilizations both inside and outside of the legal academy have arisen to control the academy's institutional and ideological development. The Crits' campaign for American law schools was not the first campaign, and it surely will not be the last.

NOTES

1. Reagan (1988).
2. Robert Gordon, "Key Ideas," *Critical Legal Studies: Intellectual History and the History of the Present*, February 28, 2020, Princeton, NJ.
3. See *Searching for Contemporary Legal Thought*, eds. Justin Desautels-Stein and Christopher Tomlins (Cambridge & New York: Cambridge University Press, 2017).
4. Cheryl Harris, "Aftermath and Legacies: A Few Critical Thoughts," *Critical Legal Studies: Intellectual History and the History of the Present*, February 28, 2020, Princeton, NJ.
5. *The Wisconsin Conference on Critical Race Theory: A Dialogue on the Role of Law in the Maintenance and Elimination of Racial Subordination*, November 9–10, 1990, Madison, WI.
6. Matsuda (2020).
7. Ibid. Also see Trubek (2011); Kimberle Williams Crenshaw, "Twenty Years of Critical Race Theory: Looking Back to Move Forward,"

Connecticut Law Review, Vol. 43, No. 5 (2011); Gary Peller, "History, Identity, and Alienation," *Connecticut Law Review*, Vol. 43, No. 5 (2011); Gearey (2013); Joel F. Handler, "Postmodernism, Protest, and the New Social Movements," *Law & Society Review*, Vol. 26, No. 4 (1992): 707–9; Tushnet (1991); Duncan Kennedy, "Intersectionality and Critical Race Theory: A Genealogical Note from a CLS Point of View," August 6, 2017. https://ssrn.com/abstract=3014312.

8. See *Class Crits: A Network for Critical Analysis of Law and Economic Inequality*. www.classcrits.org; *LatCrit: Latina & Latino Critical Legal Theory, Inc.* www.latcrit.org; Athena D. Mutua, "ClassCrits Time? Building Institutions, Building Frameworks," *Journal of Law and Political Economy*, Vol. 1, No. 2 (2021).

9. Libby Adler, *Gay Priori: A Queer Critical Legal Studies Approach to Law Reform* (Durham, NC and London: Duke University Press, 2018).

10. Aziza Ahmed, "Aftermaths and Legacies: Critical Legal Studies in Feminist and Queer Legal Theory and Law Reform," *Critical Legal Studies: Intellectual History and the History of the Present*, February 28, 2020, Princeton, NJ.

11. Matsuda (2020).

12. Karl E. Klare, Letter to Provost Robert P. Lowndes, April 4, 1990; Jessica Treadway, "Law Delegation Visits Poland, Czechoslovakia," *Northeastern University Alumni Magazine*, Vol. 15, No. 5 (1990): 9; Peter Gabel, "Left Meets East," *Tikkun*, Vol. 5, No. 3 (1990): 22–24, 93–95.

13. David Trubek, Letter to Karl Klare, March 5, 1990.

14. Ibid.

15. See, e.g., Krever, Lisberger, and Utzschneider (2015); Joanne Conaghan and Kerry Rittich, *Labour Law, Work, and Family: Critical and Comparative Perspectives* (New York: Oxford University Press, 2005); Joanne Conaghan, Richard Michael Fischl, and Karl Klare, *Labour Law in an Era of Globalization: Transformative Practices and Possibilities* (Oxford: Oxford University Press, 2002); Helena Alviar Garcia, Karl E. Klare, and Lucy A. Williams, *Social and Economic Rights in Theory and Practice* (London and New York: Routledge, 2015); Richard Michael Fischl, "Intell and the Transformation of Critical Labor Law," *Critical Legal Studies: Intellectual History and the History of the Present*, February 28, 2020, Princeton, NJ; Lucy Williams, "Aftermath and Legacies," *Critical Legal Studies: Intellectual History and the History of the Present*, February 28, 2020, Princeton, NJ.

16. Williams (2020).

17. Former leaders of the Students for a Democratic Society, "An Open Letter to the New New Left from the Old New Left," *The Nation*, April 16, 2020. https://www.thenation.com/article/activism/letter-new-

left-biden/. Also see Mitchell Abidor, "These Young Socialists Think They Have Courage. They Don't," *New York Times*, May 13, 2020.

18. Ibid.

19. Bhaskar Sunkara, "You've Probably Heard Socialists Won't Vote for Biden," *New York Times*, May 28, 2020; Joel Bleifuss, "Former Leaders of SDS, Meet the Current Members of DSA," May 27, 2020. *In These Times*. https://inthesetimes.com/article/22546/response-nat ion-old-new-left-dsa-endorsement-criticism; David Duhalde and Mike Davis, "Responses to an 'Open Letter to the New New Left,'" *The Nation*, April 27, 2020. https://www.thenation.com/article/politics/ responses-to-an-open-letter-to-the-new-new-left/; Paul Heideman, "Stop Trying to Shame Socialists into Voting for Joe Biden. It's Not Going to Work." *Jacobin*, May 14, 2020. https://jacobinmag.com/2020/ 05/joe-biden-nyt-new-york-times-mitchell-abidor-third-party-dsa; Daniel Finn, "An Open Letter from SDS Veterans Haranguing Young Socialists to Back Biden Was a Bad Idea," *Jacobin*, April 17, 2020. https://jac obinmag.com/2020/04/sds-new-left-joe-biden-letter.

20. *Critical Legal Studies: Intellectual History and the History of the Present*, February 27–28, 2020, Princeton, NJ.

21. William Forbath, "Critical Legal Studies vs. Law & Political Economy: Critique & Utopia vs. Social Democracy," *Critical Legal Studies: Intellectual History and the History of the Present*, February 28, 2020, Princeton, NJ; Jedediah Britton-Purdy, David Singh Grewal, Amy Kapczynski, and K. Sabeel Rahman, "Building a Law-and-Political-Economy Framework: Beyond the Twentieth-Century Synthesis," *Yale Law Journal*, Vol. 129, No. 6 (2020); *The Law and Political Economy Project*. https://lpeproject. org/.

22. For more on the role of support structures in legal change, see Charles R. Epp, *The Rights Revolution: Lawyers, Activists, and Supreme Courts in Comparative Perspective* (Chicago: University of Chicago Press, 1998); Hollis-Brusky and Wilson (2020).

23. Even CLS bigwig Duncan Kennedy concedes: "So in 1989, it was very clear that anti-CLS reactions in legal academia by powerful legal academics were at an all-time high and they weren't getting smaller. The consequence of that, organizationally, was that you couldn't get promoted and you couldn't get a job if you were too overtly identified with CLS. You couldn't rise within law schools, you couldn't get tenure, and you couldn't get a job. So on all these levels, there's serious pushback." Kennedy, Interview.

24. Fischl, Interview; Tushnet (1991); Binder (1987); Susan Lampert Smith, "King of 'Crits' Returns to 'Tolerant' UW," *Wisconsin State Journal*, September 27, 1987; Frug (1987).

25. Feinman and Feldman (1985), 926.

26. Schlegel (1984), 403.
27. David Trubek, Letter to Karl Klare, February 8, 1978; Mark Tushnet, Letter to Organizing Committee and Others Interested, September 22, 1982; David Kairys, "Structure of CCLS," January 28, 1983; Mark Tushnet, Letter to Organizing Committee and Others Interested, February 7, 1983.
28. Trubek, Interview. For more information on the role that financial patronage plays in the development and maintenance of effective support structures, see Hollis-Brusky and Wilson (2020).
29. Orren and Skowronek (2004), 78.
30. Paul Baumgardner, "Going Back to School: Research into Academic Politics and the Politics of Academics," *The Docket, Law and History Review*, Vol. 2, No. 2 (2019).
31. Staszak (2015), 217.
32. Jeffrey K. Tulis and Nicole Mellow, *Legacies of Losing in American Politics* (Chicago: University of Chicago Press, 2018).
33. Tulis and Mellow (2018), 135.
34. "Law Schools and Professional Education: Report and Recommendations of the Special Committee for a Study of Legal Education," *American Bar Association* (Chicago: ABA Press, 1980): 20.

INDEX

CPSIA information can be obtained
at www.ICGtesting.com
Printed in the USA
LVHW011234151221
706052LV00003BA/372